WHATEVER IT TAKES

Transforming American Schools
The Project GRAD Story

HOLLY HOLLAND

Foreword by Donna Peterson

TEACHERS
COLLEGE
PRESS

Teachers College, Columbia University
New York and London

Published by Teachers College Press, 1234 Amsterdam Avenue, New York, NY 10027

Library of Congress Cataloging-in-Publication Data

Holland, Holly.
    Whatever it takes : transforming American schools : the Project GRAD story / Holly Holland ; foreword by Donna Peterson.
        p. cm.
    Includes bibliographical references and index.
    ISBN 0-8077-4543-X (cloth : alk. paper) — ISBN 0-8077-4542-1 (pbk. : alk. paper)
    1. Project GRAD. 2. School improvement programs—United States. 3. Educational change—United States. 4. Urban high schools—United States. I. Title.
LB2822.82.H64   2004
373.173′2—dc22   2004058057

ISBN 0-8077-4542-1 (paper)
ISBN 0-8077-4543-X (cloth)

Printed on acid-free paper
Manufactured in the United States of America

12   11   10   09   08   07   06   05   8   7   6   5   4   3   2   1

WHATEVER IT TAKES

Transforming American Schools
The Project GRAD Story

To Daniel, Gabriel, Kuol,
Michael, Peter, and Shauntrice—
My family of first-generation college students

CONTENTS

PART II: SCALING UP

FOREWORD

Educators face daunting odds when trying to help all students achieve. The challenges range from large class sizes that make individualized instruction and personal connections more difficult, to high-stakes tests that expect everyone to excel in the same ways at the same time, regardless of their background or preparation. In Alaska, schools may be small, but our teachers are no less encumbered. They must be excellent in all subjects and know how to effectively manage curriculum and classes with several grade levels in one room. These expectations don't change, despite having both limited opportunities for professional development and, because of fiscal restraints, limited resources to support their work. Additional challenges include students who don't speak English, communities in economic and social crisis, schools in barely accessible locations, and 100% teacher turnover each year in some of our buildings. Because federal and state policies continue to focus accountability measures on teacher performance and certification, local school districts are left searching for effective and efficient methods of providing professional support for teachers so they can, in turn, improve student achievement.

In 2002, representatives of Project GRAD–USA met with our district leadership team and proposed a unique partnership to support our struggling schools on the Kenai Peninsula. Until that point, we had made many attempts to change the course of education in our most troubled schools. We had invested more money in programs. We had invested in people. But we hadn't tried the comprehensive approach to reform offered through Project GRAD—and now we're glad we did. Project GRAD's proven track-record in the lower 48 states was a strong selling point as we searched for a way to permanently improve our seven lowest-performing schools. But the organization's flexibility in modifying the program to meet our specific needs helped close the deal.

Through the work of the Project GRAD coaches, we now have ongoing professional development and support in each of our buildings, helping teachers and principals in these isolated locations. Project GRAD's commitment to serve as a catalyst for change in the schools and as a partner with school personnel, parents, and community members will only strengthen our effectiveness in years to come. After just one year, we are already seeing changes that will help teachers more effectively educate students.

There are moments when the months of hard work, planning, and hoping come together for a superintendent. For me, one such moment occurred in 2004 during our first Summer Institute. The Summer Institute is a Project GRAD component that helps disadvantaged high school students envision a brighter future by taking exploratory and enrichment classes on college campuses. We all recognized the value of having students experience intense, rigorous courses so that they will understand the kind of preparation that is necessary to succeed in college. However, an unexpected impact of the Project GRAD Summer Institute was the bridge of communication and caring that students from different communities built during their time together. The pride of the students, teachers, and parents was unparalleled. Their hope was palpable. And today, our students' futures seem brighter than ever. Students and parents now have stronger reasons to value education, and they have begun working with the school district in a very positive way.

Why is our experience important for an audience outside Alaska? First, whether in rural, urban, or suburban areas, everyone in education today needs help guiding disadvantaged students, whose problems can overwhelm even the most dedicated school staffs. And one insight we have gained from many years in the trenches is that we can't solve these problems alone. We need programs, resources, and supports that will help us develop a more strategic, comprehensive approach to closing the achievement gap for poor and minority students. Project GRAD offers that assistance.

Second, none of us can afford to fail. The days of allowing ourselves to succeed with some students, but not all, have become part of educational history. Whether we're trying to meet the requirements of state accountability measures or of the federal No Child Left Behind Act, school districts across the country are being judged on the ability to reach every student. As challenging as that assignment may be, the alternatives are far worse. Consider that, since 1995, states have spent more money building prisons than colleges, according to the Justice Policy Institute. And in most states it costs far more to incarcerate youths than it does to educate them. Supporting Project GRAD in our schools is a far better use of our money.

Third, successful education reform models are rare. We've all seen plenty of promising initiatives fail to flourish beyond the pilot stage. Spreading effective strategies has become as difficult as sustaining those methods. So when I heard about a school reform model that has produced positive results in a wide range of districts over a long period of time, I paid attention. Project GRAD has expanded and endured.

This book describes how Project GRAD has evolved over the past 12 years in Houston, Los Angeles, Newark, Atlanta, Knoxville, and many other cities around the country. It also highlights the process of developing the program here in Alaska. It is important to note that, while our schools are mostly rural, our students struggle with the same issues as students do in urban areas, including high dropout rates, serious levels of substance abuse, teen pregnancy, and epidemic poverty. As long as Project GRAD continues to see our relationship as a process, and works with us to raise the bar for student and teacher expectations, we look forward to a successful, long-term relationship. Students, families, and communities will be strengthened as teachers and staff are supported in their goals of all students attaining educational excellence.

—Donna Peterson, Ed. D.
Superintendent, Kenai Peninsula Borough School District

ACKNOWLEDGMENTS

I wish to express my sincere thanks to all the students, parents, teachers, principals, researchers, mentors, consultants, executive directors, board members, and others who shared their experiences with me and graciously answered my questions about Project GRAD. I have tried to represent your views honestly, thoroughly, and compassionately.

Special thanks to the Ford Foundation for providing critical financial support for this book; to Steven Zwerling and Jim Ketelsen for initiating this project; to Glee Holton and Mona Grant for their assistance in keeping the project on track; to Sam Freedman for his essential critique; to Vivian Mateo for her excellent transcription and translation services; to Robert Rivera for intervening during key points; to Will Nix for expert legal advice; and to Carole Saltz and Catherine Chandler of Teachers College Press for guiding the manuscript.

I also acknowledge Dr. Jerome Freiberg's interview and support for this work. Consistency Management & Cooperative Discipline® (CMCD®) are service and trademarks of Consistency Management Associates Inc. Dr. Freiberg has published his story and the history of the evolution of the CMCD educational methodology in Freiberg, H. J. (2003). *The History of: From Tourists to Citizens in the Classroom.* Houston: Consistency Management Associates Inc.

Finally, I wish to thank my husband, John Herzfeld, and our sons, Dylan and Treavor, for coping with my absences while I was working on this book and for providing a steady supply of love, hugs, and bad jokes.

INTRODUCTION

There are many reasons why people choose not to go to college—and all of these stifle students in America's poorest urban schools.

Lack of money is the most obvious obstacle. The average cost of tuition, adjusted for inflation, more than doubled between 1981 and 2000 at public and private colleges (Horn, Wei, & Berker, 2002). The increase represents four times the growth of median family income during that period and dwarfs gains in federal financial aid. In addition, aspiring students often cannot afford basic fees, such as the cost of college applications and admission tests, books and living expenses, or an airplane ticket back home.

Many students in urban schools lack the right academic preparation for college. In America's largest cities, public high schools graduate on average less than half the students who enter as 9th graders, according to one national study (Balfanz & Legters, 2001). Although Latino and African-American youths, who comprise the bulk of urban school populations, have improved their high school graduation and college attendance rates in the past 20 years, they still lag behind white students (Cavanagh, 2002). Black students have narrowed the gaps, particularly in high school completion rates, but the differences for Latinos persist at every level of educational attainment (U.S. Department of Education, 2000). Moreover, most of the achievement gains for Latino and black youths occurred before 1990 (Cavanagh, 2002).

On average, poor and minority 9th graders perform 3 to 4 years below grade level in reading (Joftus, 2002). They typically attend classes led by inexperienced teachers who often lack certification or a strong background in the subjects they teach. The Education Trust, a national group that advocates for poor and minority children, finds that they are twice as likely as others to have unqualified teachers (Barthe, 2000). Nationwide, one in eight teachers lacks certification, but the figure jumps to one in five in high-poverty schools (Solmon & Firetag, 2002). Such students also suffer because of the generally low expectations of their teachers and the limited number of advanced classes offered at their high schools (Snipes, Doolittle, & Herlihy, 2002).

Without skilled and demanding teachers, students rarely learn how to take appropriate notes during lectures, comprehend complicated textbook passages, write analytical research papers, manage their time to meet multiple assignment deadlines, and persist with difficult material—skills that are necessary to do well at a university. A study for the Pathways to College Network found that the strength of the high school academic program and the level of social and emotional support provided to students were the greatest predictors of success in college (Martinez & Klopott, 2002). Yet, only about one fourth of students from low-income families are enrolled in college-preparatory programs, compared to two thirds of students from high-income families (Owings, 1995).

Many urban students also don't have mentors to show them the way out of the blighted neighborhoods that have shaped their childhoods. They need people who can help them look beyond the minimum-wage jobs that are available to high school dropouts to the long-term advantages of a college degree, including the million-dollar difference in lifetime earnings (Joftus, 2002). They need regular exposure to role models, too, particularly successful professionals whose skin tones and life experiences match their own.

When they do dream of college, many urban students don't come from cultures that provide the right support. Undereducated parents who need help with the family's finances may not understand how much more their children can contribute with a college degree. Many parents also are unaware of the steps necessary to prepare their children for college, such as encouraging them to take challenging courses in high school and apply for scholarships and financial aid (Venezia, Kirst, & Antonio, n.d.). In addition, aspiring students report that resentful relatives and insecure peers often discourage their advancement because they fear being left behind.

Students who sweep these barriers aside typically discover the isolation and loneliness that come with being a trailblazer. When they reach the campuses they dared to attend, first-generation college students often harbor strong self-doubts about whether they belong. And in truth, many of them don't have the skills to succeed. While 63% of high school graduates enroll in college the following semester, only 50% of low-income students do, and half of them require remedial work that usually dooms their chances of completing a degree (Venezia et al.). Nearly 4 in 10 disadvantaged students who attempt college fail to earn a bachelor's degree, compared to about 2 in 10 from more privileged backgrounds (U.S. Department of Education, 2000). Yet low-income students who take the most rigorous high school courses earn bachelor's degrees at the same rates as students from higher income brackets (Carnevale & Fry, 2000). The difference is preparation.

This book focuses on poor and minority students who overcame the obstacles to higher education. It describes the strategies they used to succeed, explores the problems they encountered, and shares their advice for helping other disadvantaged youths get ahead.

The story also recounts one man's determination to give those students a brighter future. James L. Ketelsen, the former head of one of America's largest corporations, turned a college scholarship pledge into a national campaign to improve the education of poor and minority students.

Although it is just one of many school improvement plans circulating around the country, Ketelsen's initiative includes some distinctive features that can enlarge our understanding of what it takes to transform urban education. Because the initiative has expanded to many U.S. cities, it also provides an opportunity to discover whether successful models of urban reform can be widely exported. Finally, by trying to bring business, philanthropic, and education leaders together under one tent, the initiative demonstrates the problems and the potential of committing to a common and sustained agenda for improving public schools.

The name of the initiative is Project GRAD, which stands for Graduation Really Achieves Dreams. It works to change the culture of urban education from passive acceptance of failure to the expectation that academic success will follow every student who receives the right preparation in school. Project GRAD seeks to do that by providing what's typically missing from a disadvantaged student's education: a consistent and rigorous course of studies from elementary school through high school, safe and orderly classrooms, regular exposure to higher education, counseling and crisis intervention to solve family troubles that distract from learning, and scholarships to pay for college. This straightforward platform for educational excellence is one that students in many American schools take for granted. But for those who attend public schools in the nation's urban core, such features are neither common nor expected.

Project GRAD's reforms have helped accelerate achievement at 73 schools in Houston, where the initiative began taking shape in the late 1980s and was formalized in 1993. Project GRAD started with a single high school, Jefferson Davis, one of the lowest-performing schools in the Houston Independent School District (HISD). At the time, fewer than 40% of the 9th graders who entered Davis earned diplomas 4 years later. The school had pervasive gang violence, about 65 pregnant teenagers a year, not one Advanced Placement course that would enable students to earn college credit, and only 20 students—12% of the graduating class—pursued higher education (Opuni, 1999). Only 10% of the 11th graders scored above the national average in reading, and just 36% did so in math.

Since then, student pregnancies at Davis have declined, college enrollment has increased 62% compared to 13% for the school district as a whole, and the percentage of Davis students who graduate in 4 years has increased by about 3% a year to 75%, according to several sources, including the Texas Education Agency and the President's Advisory Commission on Educational Excellence for Hispanic Americans.[1] The graduation rate at Davis exceeds both the district average and the 54 to 59% high school completion rates for Hispanics nationally (American Council on Education, 2003; Greene, 2002). In addition, Davis High School's average annual achievement scores have risen by one third since 1994, outpacing the state's average gains but falling slightly behind the district's average gains for the same period. Moreover, these improvements occurred at a time when the student poverty rate at Davis rose by nearly one third.

State statistics show that 60% of Davis students now complete the Texas recommended course requirements for college preparatory work, a figure that is higher than both the district and state averages (Texas Education Agency, 2002). Davis graduates have earned scholarships to prestigious universities, including Princeton, Cornell, Columbia, Colgate, and Duke.[2] Hispanic students, who represent 84% of the Davis High School population, are also completing college at more than twice the rate for Latinos nationwide.

In addition, the number of Davis students earning credit for Advanced Placement and honors-level courses is rising. In 2002, 75 students, up from just six students in 1997, took 96 of the College Board's Advanced Placement (AP) exams in calculus, English composition, English literature, Spanish language, and U.S. history. Slightly more than half scored high enough to gain college credit for the courses. Nationally, only 1 of 12 urban public school students pass the AP exams (Bacon, 2003).

After Project GRAD spread to seven elementary schools and one middle school that send students to Davis High School, achievement scores at those schools also rose—tripling, in the case of Marshall Middle School—and student discipline problems plunged. The elementary schools have nearly closed the gap in reading and math between their campuses and the district and state averages.

Academic and behavioral gains have been similar at other Houston schools that joined the Project GRAD network in later years. For example, at Jack Yates High School, which primarily serves African-American students from low-income families, the number of students attending college more than doubled after the first 3 years of participating in Project GRAD (Opuni, 1999). Such progress helped Project GRAD become one of 38 school-reform programs nationwide cited by the American Youth Policy Forum for its documented academic achievement gains (James, 2001).

Project GRAD does not deserve credit alone for the improvements in Houston schools. The Houston Independent School District initiated many changes during the same period, such as aligning the curriculum with the state's academic standards, which led to notable increases in student achievement across the city. And at the school level, educators took steps independent of Project GRAD to eliminate problems. For example, former Davis High School principal Emily Cole obtained federal grants to hire an on-site coordinator of a new pregnancy education program at the school and later opened a nursery on campus so students could leave their children in a safe place while they attended classes. Such actions undoubtedly helped reduce the school's high pregnancy and dropout rates. Project GRAD acted as the major catalyst for improvements in the Houston schools it serves, however, giving hope to impoverished students who thought college was out of their reach, bringing greater consistency to schools accustomed to chaos, and improving professional development for many educators.

"That's an enormous sea change," said Dr. Susan Sclafani, who served as chief of staff for the Houston Independent School District from 1994–2000 and is now involved in education policy on a national level. She continued, "I think it was the sense of hope" that inspired people to make improvements in the formerly failing schools, "but the sense of hope doesn't increase math and reading scores. It motivates you, and motivation aligned with good instruction can increase scores."

Project GRAD prompted educational progress by adopting an attitude of doing "whatever it takes" to help disadvantaged students excel. The organization's backers take that phrase literally and have used it as a rallying cry to raise about $65 million a year nationally to train teachers, buy classroom supplies, hire tutors, recruit mentors, educate parents, send teenagers to college-prep programs—anything they could identify as necessary to improve the odds for poor and minority students. Project GRAD provides these supports not through a revolutionary new scheme but by combining educational innovations that experience has shown to be effective with disadvantaged populations.

To start, Project GRAD aligns three existing curricular models to ensure that students gain basic academic skills in well-managed classrooms:

- Success for All (SFA), a reading program developed by Dr. Robert Slavin and Nancy Madden at Johns Hopkins University. Widely used in elementary schools around the country, Success for All combines highly structured lessons and tests in reading and writing that are designed to move students to language fluency by the 4th grade.
- Math Opportunities, Valuable Experiences, and Innovative Teaching (MOVE IT) Math, an elementary school program developed by Paul and Lynn Shoecraft at the University of Houston-Victoria. MOVE IT Math uses building blocks, songs, games, and other "manipulatives" to show students the principles behind mathematics instead of asking them to memorize mathematical formulas without understanding why they work.
- Consistency Management & Cooperative Discipline® (CMCD®), a classroom management program developed by Dr. H. Jerome Freiberg at the University of Houston. CMCD involves students

in setting class constitutions, encourages engaging teaching activities, and gives children opportunities to take responsibility for their learning by applying for a series of management positions. The program is designed to give students an active role in creating a culture of cooperation that supports serious intellectual work.

All three strands include training and coaching for teachers and ongoing evaluations of students' performance. To these curricular components, Project GRAD adds two other supports for students. One bolsters their academic skills and the other addresses their social/emotional needs.

- As an incentive to stay in school, Project GRAD provides a $4,000–$6,000 scholarship to graduates who complete a college-preparatory program within 4 years and maintain a 2.5 grade-point average during high school. (Some cities offer more aid to Project GRAD scholars because of the higher cost of tuition at public universities in their states.) In addition, participating students must attend two summer institutes held on college campuses to strengthen their academic skills and expose them to higher education. They receive stipends for completing each summer institute because Project GRAD recognizes that participating might prevent them from working and contributing to their families' finances.
- The social/emotional support for students is coordinated through Communities in Schools, an on-campus social services organization that provides counseling, mentoring, and links to other non-profit agencies for children and their families. To ensure coordinated services, Communities in Schools assembles a team of teachers, administrators, and counselors to monitor the progress of every student receiving assistance. Communities in Schools also sponsors classes and programs to help parents understand how to support their children's education at home and prepare them for college.

"Unique to Project GRAD is the deliberate attempt to involve the family in the school and to help families support their children in working toward the goal of college attendance," researchers noted in a national report (Martinez & Klopott, 2002). "Project GRAD could have been simply another scholarship program, but it has developed into a multifaceted initiative designed to encourage students to attend college."

The five curricular features—reading, math, and classroom management strands, along with social services support and preparation and incentives for college—form the programmatic part of Project GRAD. Five separate features comprise the structural foundation.

First, Project GRAD works within "feeder" systems of elementary, middle, and high schools serving the same population of students. The kindergarten through 12th-grade setup stems from the recognition that while poor families move frequently, they often relocate to adjoining neighborhoods and schools. Rather than force transient students to continually adapt to new lessons and a different set of expectations, Project GRAD aims to let them pick up where they left off at their previous schools. A feeder system also reduces the burden that high student transient rates place on teachers. Children who move among Project GRAD feeder schools follow a common curriculum, which helps their teachers make proper placements instead of arbitrary assignments based on their age or assumed skills.

Second, to provide support for the instructional improvements in the school feeder system, Project GRAD forms non-profit organizations in each community that joins its network. These groups are responsible for monitoring and assisting the program's implementation, coordinating fund-raising, hiring support staff, and building a constituency for change at the local level.

Third, Project GRAD seeks to mobilize and redirect the school district's existing assets, showing schools how to use money, resources, and people more efficiently and effectively. Project GRAD costs about $500 a year for each student, which represents about 6% of the national average per-pupil expenditure for public schools. The price includes program fees, classroom resources, teacher training, local staffing, and national support. To start, school districts are supposed to pay 25% of the cost and Project GRAD the remainder, with the ratios reversed after 5 years. By persuading school districts to allocate some of the paid teacher-training days already on the schedule for Project GRAD's purposes, shift the programs that federal grants pay for, and redeploy curriculum specialists to help coach math and reading, the organization says it can cut the per-pupil costs by up to one half, so that they are not added expenditures but rather part of the regular budget for schools.

Fourth, Project GRAD collaborates with community groups. In some cases, this means turning their attention to disadvantaged children, and in other cases linking them with local groups that are trying to help public schools. For example, two public universities in Knoxville agreed to sponsor the summer college institutes for Project GRAD students and provide scholarships to graduates who are later admitted. This collaboration reduces the school district's cost of participating in Project GRAD and helps the universities meet state goals for increasing campus diversity.

Finally, Project GRAD sets up a national network of participating schools that share ideas and receive support from an organization called Project GRAD–USA. The national group formed in 2001 to coordinate Project GRAD's expansion to some of the most troubled school systems in the country, including those in Newark; Los Angeles; Atlanta; and Roosevelt, New York. By 2003, Project GRAD was working with about 130,000 students in nearly 200 schools.

"The interesting thing about the model to me is that it almost starts with some scaling up. It doesn't just start in a school; it starts with a cluster," said Leslie Graitcer, former executive director of the BellSouth Foundation and now an independent consultant in educational philanthropy. "It's much more comprehensive than I think many of the [reform] models are—it's process *and* content . . . a majority of all the other models are school reform models. The thing about Project GRAD is that it is much more about a district, that children move from school to school and we have to look at this much more comprehensively."[3]

Spearheading school reform in the nation's urban core is not for the fainthearted, as Project GRAD's experience shows. The national rollout of Project GRAD has produced problems along with opportunities. Nevertheless, these issues are instructive because they help explain why urban school reform has been so spotty and short-lived. In addition, Project GRAD's expansion provides insights about the steps that promising models of educational change must take to successfully spread their influence.

Through a combination of naïveté, urgency, and arrogance, Project GRAD's directors agreed to export their model before they understood the vagaries of state and local politics, the depth of fear and resistance among educators who work in America's inner cities, and the limitations of the programs and trainers they offered to those sites. Inflexible union rules, state testing and curricular changes, turnover among superintendents and school administrators, and the high cost of providing services to far-flung organizations—Project GRAD initially underestimated the impact of these and other impediments to successful expansion beyond Houston. In their rush to implement the model on a national scale, Project GRAD's developers also forgot sometimes to focus on forming strong relationships with the people they aimed to help.

For example, Nashville and Project GRAD discontinued their partnership by mutual agreement in 2002. Although Nashville was among the first cities to join the national network in 1999, its arrangement with Project GRAD was tenuous from the start. Vanderbilt University, not a separate non-profit organization, coordinated all the local activities. In addition, the district announced that some of the schools within the Project GRAD feeder system would be closed because of consolidation. Local organizers also disliked some of the curricular components and training provided by Project GRAD, so teachers didn't adopt most of the features. As a result, Project GRAD–Nashville reorganized in the summer of 2002 and assumed a new name.

In Newark and Los Angeles, local supporters expressed frustration that Project GRAD initially ignored their advice about how to adapt the reform model to fit their communities, which resulted in lukewarm support from some educators and philanthropists. New superintendents in Columbus and Los Angeles sought to substitute their preferred reading programs, and Newark schools stuck with their existing math program, causing some observers to ask whether cities should be considered part of the Project GRAD network if they don't adopt all of its components.

Critics also contend that Project GRAD has not consented to rigorous evaluations by unaffiliated groups and that its students have not achieved as well as their peers served by competing college-access programs, such as Advancement Via Individual Determination (AVID), a college-preparatory program for low-income, underachieving students that was started in 1980 by San Diego high school teacher Mary Catherine Swanson. AVID serves more than 70,000 students in 20 U.S. states and 14 countries. Reports show that about 95% of AVID's graduates enroll in college and more than 80% remain enrolled in college 2 years after admission (James, 2001).

Dr. Uri Treisman is one who believes that Project GRAD releases selective achievement data that masks the mixed experience of its schools. For example, state reports show that just 4% of Davis students completed advanced courses during the 2000–01 school year, the latest year for which statistics are available. That same year, only 46% of Davis graduates took college admission exams, down from 64% who did so in 1992, the first year students were eligible for the scholarship program that led to the formation of Project GRAD. Moreover, while the school's average SAT score rose substantially in the past decade, outpacing both district and state gains, the figure still falls below the minimally acceptable score for competitive college admissions.

"I have sympathy for the challenge of working in some of the cities they've chosen to work in. That's a big plus that they've taken these on," said Treisman, a math professor and director of the Charles A. Dana Center, an education research organization at the University of Texas at Austin. "I really support and believe in the core stuff. That doesn't mean they're doing it effectively."

In response to some of the identified problems and criticisms, Project GRAD made adjustments that ultimately strengthened the organization and its programs; produced quicker improvements in newer cities, such as Atlanta and Knoxville; and prompted the state of Ohio to adopt Project GRAD as the school reform model for its eight largest cities. Over time, Project GRAD refined its curricular offerings, added supports specific to certain cities, and clarified the requirements for new sites to join. The organization also raised substantial sums from private and public sources, including a total of $47 million from the U.S. Department of Education and $42 million from the Ford Foundation.

Balancing pragmatism with theory is necessary when you're trying to turn around schools and students almost no one believes can succeed. "It's not the kids," Project GRAD founder James L. Ketelsen likes to say about the problems of urban education. It's the adults, or rather their attitudes and actions, that must change.

Strong school communities create the conditions for high achievement. That's the essential message of Project GRAD and the fullest measure of its impact. Students rarely falter when surrounded by adults who believe in their potential. Parents who learn the importance of advocating for their children's education, students who learn the importance of becoming knowledgeable and responsible citizens, teachers who learn the importance of setting high standards and providing engaging instruction—these are the building blocks of effective schools.

"I think Mr. Ketelsen has demonstrated that you can improve learning in urban school districts if you do certain things: develop consistent academic programs, train people in how to use them, create incentives and support for staff and students, and develop a belief that everyone can be successful," said Robert Stockwell, chief academic officer for the Houston Independent School District. He continued: "I think because of [Project] GRAD's growing prominence, the question has to be, can you scale this up? People say this about companies and school districts. Is its success the outgrowth of leadership or the organization? In other words, is it the way the leader leads or the infrastructure? I believe it's both."

THE URBAN CONUNDRUM

Why do so many urban public schools lack the qualities for sustained progress? For the past 2 decades local, state, and national leaders have been trying—with minimal success—to answer that question.

Changing superintendents is one approach that big cities have used. Some communities have turned to leaders from non-education backgrounds, such as former army general John Stanford in Seattle and former city budget director Paul Vallas in Chicago. Other cities have tried privatization, hiring companies such as the Edison Schools Inc. to shake up district bureaucracies. Some cities, such as San Diego, have abided by state requirements permitting charter schools to operate alongside district-controlled schools. Others, such as Cleveland and Milwaukee, have lost money and students to private schools through vouchers. To bring instructional consistency to urban classrooms, some cities have adopted packaged school reforms, ranging from E.D. Hirsch's Core Knowledge, which expects students to know prescribed facts and skills at each grade level, to the Galef Institute's Different Ways of Knowing, which promotes adaptable tools and targeted coaching to help schools meet their specific improvement plans.

A few urban schools have managed to break away from the pack of poor performers, but their successes rarely last. Many of the notable practices stem from the work of dynamic principals and faculties whose initiatives fade when they leave. One national study referred to these isolated examples as "islands of excellence" in a desolate sea (Togneri & Anderson, 2003).

This is not to say that urban schools haven't made progress. Research from the Council of Great City Schools, which represents the nation's largest urban districts, shows that two thirds of big-city school districts posted gains in math at every grade level from 2000 to 2002, although reading scores remained flat (Reid, 2003). Between 2002 and 2003, 90% of the 4th graders tested in 61 urban school districts improved their test scores in math, and 93% did so in reading. Among 8th graders, 83% improved in math, but only 53% did so in reading (Gewertz, 2004). The average ACT composite score among the nation's largest urban school districts also did not change from 1990 to 1999 (Council of the Great City Schools, 2001). In general, improvements across urban school districts have been inconsistent and incremental, and the different ways that schools measure achievement makes broad comparisons impossible (Snipes, Doolittle, & Herlihy, 2002).

Simultaneous with district-level reforms, states have been busy with their own agendas for educational change, a process that "is fundamentally about improving urban public schools" (Snipes, Doolittle, & Herlihy, 2002). The national movement to force public school change started with *A Nation at Risk*, the 1983 influential report from the National Commission on Excellence in Education, which warned that the relatively low achievement levels in the United States would hurt the country's international competitiveness. Among other things, the report recommended increasing the number and rigor of high school courses required for graduation (U.S. Department of Education, 2003).

In the late 1980s, the National Governors Association lent credence to *A Nation at Risk* by urging states to give school districts more flexibility in planning instruction in exchange for greater accountability for students' academic performance. President George H. W. Bush met with the governors in 1989 at the first National Education Summit, and together they set goals for public schools.

Researchers noted that "[w]hen the publication of *A Nation at Risk* jump-started the drive to reshape the nation's schools, educators viewed reform as an event, a one-time activity that would fix the problems and then recede. Sixteen years later, reform has become a permanent part of the educational landscape" (Coffey & Lashway, 2002). Further, "educators once viewed reform as cyclical; every 10 years or so, one could expect an outburst of public concern, followed by frenetic efforts to mend the system, followed by a return to the status quo. In the last two decades, however, that dependable cycle has been upset, and schools now seem to be in a perpetual state of restructuring."

During the 1990s, states began setting common academic standards for students in every school district and establishing benchmarks that all children must reach, as measured by annual standardized tests. Yet attaining higher goals has proven more difficult than envisioning them. As Harvard Education Professor Richard F. Elmore (2002) notes,

> From the beginning, performance-based accountability was a strictly *political* idea, designed to bring a broad coalition together behind a single vision of reform. As with most such ideas, it was weak on practical details, most of which were left to state and local policymakers and educators. (p. 35)

The school accountability movement became more complicated in 2001 when the federal government, through the No Child Left Behind Act, began requiring states to test students annually in grades 3 through 8 and to break down the scores according to students' race and family income. The federal government further demanded that states demonstrate over time that all students could reach defined proficiency levels, as measured by standardized tests.

The impact of all these changes on urban schools has not been as bold as promised. Elementary school scores have risen slowly, but high school scores have not. The schools most often targeted for special assistance or sanctions for failing to show progress reside in low-income communities.

The most troublesome aspect of the weak system of urban public schools is that so many students never get to experience educational excellence. Their futures are effectively circumscribed the minute their families move into one of hundreds of inner-city neighborhoods across the country. As a sobering new study from Johns Hopkins University reports:

- Almost half of black students and 40% of Latino students (compared to 11% of white students) attend high schools where most of those who enroll never graduate.
- During the 1990s, the number of U.S. high schools with high dropout and low graduation rates rose by 75%.
- In nearly 3,000 U.S. high schools, 40–50% of the freshmen drop out before they reach the 12th grade (Balfanz & Legters, 2004).

"In some cities, students have virtually no other choice but to attend a high school with weak promoting power," the Johns Hopkins researchers concluded (p. 2).

As these statistics make clear, it is more important than ever that the United States find solutions to the problems in urban education. Behind those numbers are real teenagers who need real hope of a productive future, which comes from a solid educational foundation. Studying successful interventions, such as Project GRAD, thus becomes a national necessity, not merely an academic exercise.

Elmore concludes,

Low-performing schools aren't coherent enough to respond to external demands for accountability. . . . The work of turning a school around entails improving "capacity" (the knowledge and skills of teachers)—changing their command of content and how to teach it—and helping them to understand where their students are in their academic development. Low-performing schools, and the people who work in them, don't know what to do. If they did, they would be doing it already.

Washington Post columnist Neal R. Peirce (2002), who specializes in urban issues, further explains that big-city school systems have tended to focus on repetitive test-taking skills instead of improving the conditions for learning. In their push for higher scores and quick solutions to longstanding problems, state and district leaders have "barely scratched the surface of creating true community-based schools that integrate after-hours services such as health, mental health, recreation, library, and continuing education for the 'whole kid' and his family. Without that integration, school outcomes may never improve much. The secret lies in combining high standards with personal attention to kids and families in troubled neighborhoods."

§   §   §

The multifaceted approach that Peirce describes is what Project GRAD uses with high-poverty schools, and the reason I became interested in writing about the initiative. As a journalist specializing in education issues, I have observed a broad range of schools across the country and have spent considerable time in classrooms that variously intrigued, bored, frightened, and amazed me. In the past 15 years, I have tracked school improvement efforts initiated by state legislatures, foundations, corporations, private consultants, public advocacy groups, and hard-charging educators. Each time I came away from the experience with a fuller understanding of why such undertakings succeed or fail.

In 2002, when the Ford Foundation asked me to take a look at an urban school reform initiative that it had backed for 6 years, I was skeptical of what I would see. But that spring, when I traveled to Houston to visit the first feeder system to participate in Project GRAD, I left impressed. Instead of the dispirited and disruptive schools I often see in inner-city neighborhoods, I found students who were engaged and attentive in orderly, colorful, almost joyful classrooms. Not every teacher provided scintillating instruction, but most of them held the children's attention and followed a carefully sequenced and challenging curriculum. At the middle school and high school level, there were gaps in the program, with a few teachers continuing to rely on monotone lectures and simplistic exercises to fill long class periods. Yet for the most part, the schools emitted an infectious buzz of learning, and students openly affirmed their interest in being there.

As I widened my exploration to include other Project GRAD schools, both in Houston and around the country, I found similarly persuasive settings but also pockets of problems. In some cases, caustic conversations between and among students and adults confirmed that new attitudes and expectations had not penetrated the traditionally harsh climates in urban public schools. In other cases, I saw that many educators had made only minimal changes to their leadership and instructional routines, a sign that the training and support provided by Project GRAD was either inadequate or incomplete.

Throughout my examination of the Project GRAD schools, leaders at both the Ford Foundation and Project GRAD were eager to learn from my observations. They invited me to attend their meetings, they shared internal studies and documents, and they willingly fulfilled my requests for information and interviews. They did provide their own interpretation of events and, occasionally, sought to deflect criticism. Unless otherwise noted, however, the analysis and conclusions in the book are based on my independent review.

PART I

A PLAN FOR POOR KIDS

Chapter 1

BUILDING A COMMUNITY
OF LEARNERS

Project GRAD unofficially started in the spring of 1988 when a group of corporate executives invited Davis High School principal Emily Cole to lunch. After just a few weeks at her new job at Davis, Cole ventured to the 30-story office tower occupied by Tenneco Inc., a major energy and manufacturing conglomerate whose headquarters were in Houston. Cole entered the building's lobby and spotted three elevators, one with a gold door. The opulent entrance led to the building's top floor and opened onto a luxurious two-story atrium with an indoor garden and a cascading wall of water. Six large enclosed meeting rooms framed the floor and waiters bustled in and out of the executive dining room.

Cole, whose high school didn't have a cafeteria, was both dazzled and overwhelmed. What brought her back to reality was the following question from her hosts: "What are you going to do about Davis?"

Tenneco, it turns out, had been actively supporting Davis High School since 1981. The run-down, two-story brick building was located in Houston's Near North Side, an impoverished neighborhood that skirts the downtown skyline but shares none of its political and economic power. Just 44% of the adults in the Davis community had completed high school. Most of the residents had emigrated from Mexico and Central America, spoke little English, and supported large families through physical labor. In 1988, the year Cole came to Davis, only 175 of the 600 students who entered 4 years earlier as freshmen had earned diplomas. Twenty of those graduates subsequently enrolled in college, and only four of them ultimately obtained college degrees (O'Connell, 2002).

At first, Tenneco provided a traditional school-business partnership with employees mentoring and tutoring students. Two years later, Tenneco acted as the catalyst for getting Communities in Schools (CIS), a dropout prevention program, to coordinate on-site social services at Davis. Tenneco also awarded two $10,000 college scholarships to the school's top graduates and spearheaded physical improvements in the building, including replacing windows, painting woodwork, and renovating the auditorium.

In 1985, Tenneco stepped up its efforts by sponsoring a summer leadership-training program for selected Davis students. For 3 years, the company also took any Davis teacher who was willing to a special summer staff-development retreat at a Texas resort. In 1985, Tenneco's assistance to Davis earned the company the Presidential Award for Private Sector Initiatives, and with it, recognition as the nation's most comprehensive school-business partnership.

Tenneco executives saw untapped potential at Davis. Through actions that were both altruistic and pragmatic, they were trying to keep Houston's underclass from a lifetime of crime and economic dependence that would reduce the city's educated workforce and limit its appeal to investors.[1]

In those days (the company sold most of its assets to the El Paso Corporation in 1996), Tenneco was a big, swaggering company with products ranging from polyvinyl chloride to nuclear submarines. It rarely backed down from a challenge. So when the Houston school district brought the company a list of possible partnership schools, Tenneco picked a place with the highest odds.

"I said, 'The one that I'm going to adopt is not offered,'" recalled Jo Swinney McLaughlin, who was Tenneco's community affairs director and later director of the Tenneco Foundation, through which most of the financial assistance to the school passed. "'What do you mean?' they said. 'I said, I want Jeff Davis.'"

Through Tenneco, McLaughlin had initiated community development efforts in many areas of Houston, including starting a literacy program in one of the public housing complexes that sent children to Davis. She knew from those experiences that educators couldn't teach poor students unless they had help resolving the family crises that often kept the children from learning. That was the major reason she wanted Communities in Schools at Davis.

Throughout the decade, Tenneco also collaborated with business, government, and nonprofit groups to provide summer jobs for Davis students, encouraging them to stay in school while helping them see career possibilities. Tenneco guaranteed the students' $600 salaries for 6 weeks of work. In 1988, Tenneco started a summer "bridge" program to smooth the transition from middle school to high school for rising 9th graders. In addition, about 200 employees at a time volunteered at the school.

The trouble was, the tremendous assistance Tenneco provided to Davis didn't seem to matter. When Chairman and Chief Executive Officer James L. Ketelsen asked his employees to provide evidence that their efforts had helped, they couldn't supply the data. Everyone felt good about Tenneco's involvement with Davis, but no one could point to lower dropout rates, higher test scores, or any other measurable changes at the school. Ketelsen, an accountant by training who was accustomed to reviewing spreadsheets with cost-earnings ratios, wanted tangible results.

"Our people couldn't come back with anything that showed improvements," he said. "At that point, I said, 'Well, let's try something else.'"

Ketelsen was no stranger to the difficulties of school reform. From the time he became chairman of Tenneco in 1978 until he retired in 1991, he led a series of private sector initiatives to improve the conditions of underserved populations. He also enlisted about 1,500 Tenneco employees, retirees, and family members in support of those efforts. The October 17, 1983 issue of *Industry Week* magazine honored Ketelsen with its Excellence in Management Award for public service (Modic, 1983).

Ketelsen embodied the community connections he expected his employees to make, devoting about one third of his professional and personal time to philanthropy (Modic, 1983). He served on the national Committee for Economic Development, which completed a compelling study of urban education. He provided leadership and support to the Houston Committee for Private Sector Initiatives. And his work with the national Business Roundtable and the Texas Business and Education Coalition would put Texas in the forefront of the country's push for greater school accountability.

In spite of these efforts, however, Ketelsen hadn't been able to change the circumstances of a single urban high school that his company had been assisting at the rate of about $400,000 annually for nearly a decade (Hodge, 2001).

In January 1989, while he was considering the next moves for the Tenneco-Davis partnership, Ketelsen attended the presidential inauguration of his fellow Texan, George H. W. Bush. On the plane ride back to Houston, Ketelsen told his wife, Kathryn, that he had been inspired by Bush's "thousand points of light" speech and pledge to be the nation's "education president." Ketelsen wondered if he could emulate that statesmanship back home. He was convinced that the achievement gap between "the haves and have-nots . . . was a problem that needed everybody's attention."

Ketelsen had heard about Eugene Lang, an East Coast businessman and philanthropist who in 1981 had "adopted" a group of New York City 6th graders from poor families and pledged to send them all to college if they graduated from high school. His promise led to the creation of the "I Have a Dream" Foundation, which spawned 180 similar scholarship projects in 27 states. Perhaps he could use the same approach with the Davis students, Ketelsen thought, promising a college scholarship to each of that year's graduates.

"He had me run some numbers and said, 'If we put a scholarship program in there, what impact would it have?'" recalled Ketelsen's former executive assistant, Barry Morris. Ketelsen wanted to know "What numbers of kids are graduating now? How many are coming into ninth grade? How many are going on to 10th grade? How many are going to college? If we guarantee a scholarship, what will it cost the company?"

Believing he could make a significant difference with the college scholarships, Ketelsen pushed ahead with his plan. He was prepared to invest an additional $200,000 to help the Davis graduates.

The closer he got to publicly announcing Tenneco's commitment, however, the closer Emily Cole and Jo McLaughlin got to panic. For her part, Cole didn't want to seem ungrateful or to alienate a man whose interest in the Davis students was becoming a personal crusade. While she recognized the advantages of expanding the school's partnership with Tenneco, she feared that promising a college scholarship to students with a meager education would be like offering a banquet to someone who's too sick to eat.

"They wanted to give the original Tenneco scholarships to the seniors, and I thought, there is absolutely no way," Cole said. "You're going to be throwing your money away. They're not prepared. They weren't academically ready for college at all."

To do well on college entrance exams, such as the SAT, students should have completed at least algebra II and rigorous English courses (Bell-Rose et al., 1998). Indeed, the SAT's top scorers nationally in every race and gender group take calculus and honors English. Moreover, research from the U.S. Department of Education shows that the level of mathematics students complete in high school is the single strongest factor in whether they earn a bachelor's degree. Students who finish a math course beyond algebra II earn college degrees at twice the rate of other students. The quality of the high school curriculum has a significantly stronger impact on the college completion rates of African-American and Latino students than for white students (Adelman, 1999).

Most students in the United States take college entrance exams at the end of their junior year in high school so they will have the results—and time to retake the exams, if necessary—to meet application deadlines during the fall semester of their senior year. When Davis students took the college entrance exams, however, most had not advanced beyond geometry because they had started with pre-algebra or remedial math in the 9th grade, followed by algebra in the 10th grade. At the time, only about 30 of the school's 1,600 students completed algebra II each year.

Like Cole, McLaughlin had serious misgivings about the Davis students' preparation for college, but she also kept quiet because she was the first woman among the senior managers at Tenneco. Previously, she had been chastised by one of her supervisors for promoting collaboration. "Take that word, *network*, out of your vocabulary," the supervisor told her. "That is a female word." Tenneco's autocratic, male-dominated executive branch made her tentative about challenging the wisdom of the CEO's plan for Davis.

Then, one weekend close to the May 1989 announcement of the scholarship offer, McLaughlin realized she had to voice her concerns. She contacted several people who had been working on the scholarship deal, and the following Monday morning she took a new plan to her supervisor at Tenneco. Instead of awarding college scholarships to the graduating seniors in 1989, the new proposal suggested offering them to 9th graders who agreed to attend two summer institutes at the University of Houston's downtown campus, maintain a 2.5 grade-point average in college preparatory classes, and graduate in 4 years. Although McLaughlin worried that Ketelsen would object to the changes, the executive to whom she reported assured her that the CEO would love the plan. And he did.

In addition to Tenneco, the new Jefferson Davis Educational Collaborative included the University of Houston-Downtown, The Metropolitan Organization (TMO), Communities in Schools, and the Houston Independent School District. From Tenneco, Ketelsen pledged up to $4,000 for college ($1,000 for each successful year of high school) to every graduate in the Davis class of 1992 and limited financial assistance to Davis students who graduated in 1989, 1990, and 1991. To give the high school students time on a college campus and special summer classes to prepare them for postsecondary education, the university created the Jesse H. Jones Summer Institute, funded by the Houston Endowment, Inc., a charitable trust. Tenneco agreed to provide $150 stipends to every student who completed the summer institute. TMO, a coalition of local churches, signed on to help the students' families understand how to prepare their children for college. And the school district paid for the position of a scholarship coordinator to help the Davis students fulfill their academic obligations.

When the Davis High School scholarship program started, tuition, books, and fees at public universities in Texas cost about $2,200 a year. At $1,000 a year, the Tenneco scholarship would cover about half the amount, less if a student lived on campus and needed to pay room and board. The hope was that the Tenneco grant would give students an incentive to try college and, with assistance from counselors and scholarship coordinators, motivation to seek additional financial aid.

To lay the groundwork for the scholarship program, Cole knew she had to get the community's support, particularly in persuading Davis parents that college was a viable option for their children. But the regular Parent Teacher Organization meetings at Davis drew half a dozen parents at most, and Cole hadn't found an effective way to bring families into the school. When she asked McLaughlin for advice, the Tenneco executive put her in touch with Robert Rivera, TMO's lead community organizer in Houston.

Rivera, a second-generation Mexican-American who had grown up in the Davis neighborhood, had extensive experience helping poor, immigrant people band together to redress inequities in government and business services. TMO was an offshoot of the Industrial Areas Foundation, a national group founded in 1940 by grassroots political organizer Saul Alinsky, who focused his community-building efforts on the urban poor (Shirley, 1997).

In Houston, TMO representatives had met with Ketelsen at Tenneco to press for lower utility costs and other concerns. Despite its radical political agenda of helping impoverished people collectively stand up for their rights, TMO had earned a reputation with Ketelsen and other Tenneco executives as a hard-working group that did its homework and demanded accountability, from the poor citizens it represented to the corporate and government entities they challenged. TMO had also formed a partnership with the Houston Independent School District to increase parental involvement at three middle schools wracked by racial tensions (Shirley, 1997).

With a grant from Tenneco to help boost parent involvement at Davis, TMO spread out into the community, building allies among leaders such as Father Tom Sheehy of Holy Name Catholic Church, the spiritual center of Houston's Near North Side. (He is now deceased.) While Father Sheehy worked discussions about college into his sermons and during his frequent visits to Davis, Cole took the same message to faculty meetings, community centers, grocery stores, and elementary schools in the neighborhood.

To explain the mostly foreign concept of college to the Davis families, Rivera recommended an approach that TMO had used in some of its previous organizing efforts—knocking on people's doors and meeting them in their homes. The plan sounded great in theory, Cole thought. But as she scanned the list of the 600 9th graders enrolled at Davis, she wondered how she and the other organizers would ever reach that many homes.

Rivera acknowledged that he had never tackled such an ambitious project before, but he reasoned that the same principles for building community support applied no matter how big the group. In his experience, it was necessary to make contact with people at least five times—through phone calls, mailings, mass media, public meetings, and face-to-face encounters—before they would agree to support an initiative, in this case the college scholarship program.

Preparations for the door-to-door campaign got underway in the fall of 1989, including recruiting 200 volunteers—many of them bilingual—and making public service announcements in both English and Spanish. Cole was bombarded with inquiries from media outlets interested in the effort to get poor kids to college. She felt pressured to fill up the school's 900-seat auditorium for the public rally scheduled a few days after the neighborhood canvas, which she dubbed the "Walk for Success."

The initial event took place on a Saturday morning in February 1990. Volunteers reached most of the freshmen's homes, and the following Tuesday Cole opened the school for an evening rally. Knowing that representatives from the media, the school board, and all the sponsoring groups would be on hand for the ceremony, she waited anxiously, hoping that the families would show up, too. "And they started arriving, and arriving, and arriving," she later said with a mixture of pride and disbelief.

A group of business, education, and religious leaders made short speeches to start the event, but it was Father Sheehy who turned the community rally into a revival. Standing at the front of the stage and speaking to families who had sought his counsel many times before, the priest urged them not to let this opportunity slip from their grasp. "Look at what these people want to do for our students," he said. "Isn't it wonderful?"

The families stood and cheered. Then, María Cantú, a Mexican-American homemaker whom Rivera had recruited during one of his visits to the neighborhood, walked to the microphone. Speaking in Spanish, she told the audience that she had not been able to attend college and was hopeful that her son, Juan, the youngest of eight children, would get that chance. Although Juan earned good grades at Davis, he was headstrong and his mother feared she would lose him to the dangerous street life (Shirley, 1997). Turning to her son, Cantú reminded Juan that she would always stand in his corner no matter what path he followed. Although she didn't want to pressure him, she hoped he would accept the challenge from Tenneco to stay in school.

"We gave you love and discipline," she said, "but we cannot send you to college. These people want to send you to college."

Juan promised to abide by the college scholarship agreement. His mother repeated her pledge of support. Then mother and son embraced and walked off the stage to thunderous applause. Afterward, three other families came up on the stage to make similarly moving testimonials.

Then Sheehy returned to the microphone and unfurled a long white scroll. "Those of you who want to be part of this," he said, "those of you who want your children to go to college, come and sign this scroll."

From the center and both side aisles, the families rushed forward. "I thought those parents were going to run over each other to commit their child to graduate and go to college," McLaughlin said. "Tears were rolling."

After the rally, Cole took the scroll with hundreds of signatures affixed and hung the unconventional contract in the school's front hallway. For many years, the scroll served as a visual reminder of the commitments the various partners had made on that memorable evening (Shirley, 1997).

Davis High School wasn't transformed that night or in the few weeks and months after. It took many years and much commitment from students, staff, and parents to significantly improve instruction and learning, to figure out what was necessary to get more students to college besides money. Cole brought in new faculty members, shook up the school's schedule, and started meeting with the principals of schools that sent students to Davis. She found meaningful roles for volunteers to play in the school and kept Tenneco informed of problems and progress. Most importantly, she inspired her mostly immigrant students to follow her path and become the first in their families to earn a college degree.

"My teenagers at Davis had other issues than just being teenagers," Cole explained. "Life is tough, very tough for some of them, and you either succumb and dig a hole or you get in there and fight for a better life."

FIRST-GENERATION COLLEGE STUDENTS

To understand how much ground the students and staff at Davis had to cover, it's helpful to trace the experiences of students in the class of 1992, the first to receive the $4,000 college scholarships from Tenneco. Consider Griselda Mani, who crossed the border between Mexico and Texas in 1985 with her older brother, Albert, joining their father, mother, and younger siblings, who had already moved to Houston. At 10 years of age, Griselda had advanced so rapidly in Mexican schools that she was supposed to start the 8th grade that fall. Instead, guidance counselors enrolled her in the 6th grade at Marshall Middle School, located across the street from Davis High School. They took one look at the diminutive girl with a voice a few decibels short of a whisper and placed her in the grade where, chronologically, she belonged.

"I always remember my first day [at Marshall] because it was so rough," she said. "I went to lunch and I had no idea what to do. And I couldn't ask people because I didn't speak English."

In math class that day, Griselda correctly answered all the problems written on the chalkboard. But when the teacher asked her follow-up questions, she was unable to respond. Numbers can cross language barriers, she discovered, but conversations can't. "She kept expecting an answer from me," Griselda said. "My eyes just filled with tears and I started crying, so she sent me out of class."

Gradually she learned English, but her limited language skills kept her from making her customary academic progress. Although Griselda attended English as a Second Language (ESL) classes at Marshall, the teachers generally didn't speak Spanish.

"Like my home economics class," she recalled. "I got a [grade of] sixty-five in there because I had no idea what to do, and everything was written in English. I did the minimum I could do because I didn't know how. I was very shy and so that didn't help."

When she moved to Davis High School, Griselda continued playing catch-up. Her high school guidance counselor reviewed her records in the 10th grade and recommended that Griselda move out of ESL classes and into the school's honors program. The decision not only helped her improve her grade-point average and class standing; it gave her a chance to consider college.

As part of the requirement for the Tenneco scholarship, Griselda attended the summer institute at the University of Houston-Downtown, where she took a preparatory class for advanced algebra. As a junior, she was among a small group of students who took trigonometry at Davis. But when she was a senior, she had reached the end of the line mathematically. The school offered no higher-level courses.

Pat Notaro, a Davis counselor, brought Griselda to the University of Houston-Downtown, where she passed a trigonometry exam that qualified her for calculus. During her senior year, she took classes at Davis during the morning and afternoon, then pursued calculus at the university in the evenings. She was the only student in her graduating class to take calculus.

Griselda hoped that her skills would lead to a career in engineering. She credits her sophomore geometry teacher, Ruth Kravetz, for showing her the way. Kravetz had recruited Griselda and four other students to participate in the Junior Engineering Technical Society design competition at the University of Houston. Working with Kravetz and another adviser, the students developed an electronic page-turner for disabled people. The group met faithfully after school for several months to perfect the design and write and practice the presentation.

"Up to that point, she had been an honors geek in geometry," Kravetz said about Griselda. But through the engineering competition, "she got to be in charge of a project and hang out with a teacher on a regular basis," which built her confidence.

Kravetz continued mentoring Griselda, including taking her to Rice University, a small, highly regarded school located in an upscale suburb of Houston. Kravetz had earned an engineering degree from Rice. Although the university was just 20 minutes by car from Griselda's home, the teenager had never seen nor heard of the school.

Because Kravetz recognized Griselda's potential and wanted her to reach as far as she could academically, she said she "almost forced" the girl to apply to Harvard University. However, with a composite SAT score of 1,060 and advanced classes only in math, Griselda didn't have the right qualifications for the Ivy League.

Rice admitted her, but Griselda's struggles were far from over. The first obstacle was figuring out how to pay for an education at an expensive private school. The $1,000-a-year scholarship from Tenneco didn't come close to covering the $17,200 annual costs at Rice. "I started applying for scholarships," Griselda said. "I almost didn't know what the word tuition meant."

Because she had not yet attained citizenship in the United States, she was ineligible for some of the scholarships she sought. Her parents hired a lawyer to speed the citizenship process and bought a typewriter to help her with scholarship essays—both expensive contributions from a large family with a limited income. Griselda eventually obtained enough scholarships, grants, and financial aid to cover all of her costs at Rice.

Although neither of her parents had attended school beyond the elementary grades, Griselda said they encouraged their children's educational aspirations. Nevertheless, they balked at letting their oldest daughter move across town to live in a campus dormitory. Traditionally, Latino families expect girls to live at home until marriage, which is why many Davis students continue to commute to college even today.

"They were afraid to let her go. They were nervous about her being on her own," said Notaro who, along with Kravetz, met with the family on several occasions to persuade them that their daughter would have a better chance of succeeding at Rice if she lived on campus.

"My parents weren't all comfortable or right with the idea," Griselda explained, but they finally realized that "I would have everything there that I needed—computers and all the resources on campus."

Living away from home for the first time was only one of many adjustments as she moved from high school to college. When Griselda started at Rice, she also experienced unexpected difficulties in the classroom. One of the cruelest lessons she absorbed in college was how widely academic standards vary among high schools. She said, "I wasn't prepared. What happened also was that I didn't *know* I wasn't ready."

She had signed up for a full schedule of classes, including a sophomore-level math class, "Differential Equations," which proved so challenging that she dropped it and repeated the second half of calculus that she had first taken at the University of Houston-Downtown. And though Griselda had passed a physics course in high school, she realized after the first physics lecture at Rice that, "Oh, my goodness, that's like all I learned the whole *year*" at Davis. "People told me that Rice was going to be hard, but I didn't know to what extent. I thought I was smart. I wasn't used to asking for help."

She earned a D in physics that first semester, which pulled her grade-point average down to 2.6, a C+/B–, for the year. These were not the high marks that Griselda had come to expect.

Her eldest brother, Albert, had earned an associate's degree from a technical school, but no one in her family had ever been to a university, so they could not understand the challenges she faced. The only person from Davis who kept in touch with her during college was Kravetz, the teacher/ mentor who called her regularly to check on her progress. About this, Griselda commented, "It's always a good feeling to know that people who have no reason to care, care. That's how her keeping in touch helped."

Ten years had passed when Griselda reconstructed her high school experiences for a reporter. Sitting in a restaurant after work as a computer software engineer and wearing a sophisticated business suit, she looked nothing like the timid teenager she described. She spoke English without an accent and recounted how she served as a role model for a large group of relatives and friends who were intent on following her to college.

A year later, Griselda Mani embarked on a different quest, returning once more to school. In July 2003, she quit the software company where she had worked since graduating from college. The next month, at the age of 28, she entered medical school at the University of Texas-Houston.

"I had an interest [in becoming a physician] in high school, but I got a little scared and discouraged at the time," Griselda explained. "Not too many people had encouraging things to say about it. All that was really stressed was how long and how hard it would be. It's the same now [but] it just doesn't scare me. I'm not intimidated anymore."

INTERNAL IMPROVEMENTS

In the early years of the Tenneco scholarship program, the obstacles that Griselda Mani and other students encountered in college weren't immediately obvious because so few of the Davis graduates had attempted to earn bachelor's degrees. The students that Tenneco and its partners were trying to help had complex challenges to overcome, from suppressed expectations that flow from poor neighborhoods to weak academic preparation that even the brightest students receive in neglected urban schools. Those gaps didn't close with the arrival of a $4,000 check for college.

Beyond school and family issues—or sometimes because of them—students living in high-poverty areas tend to experience a wide range of risky behaviors that can lead to teenage pregnancy, crime, or drug and alcohol abuse (Lippman et al., 1996). Such students often suffer from disabling health conditions or have to care for ailing relatives. All of these factors can derail an education. Students in impoverished neighborhoods are also more likely to spend limited time on homework, to watch excessive amounts of television, and to have part-time jobs that interfere with studying. Compared with other students, they have a much higher risk of performing poorly on standardized tests and dropping out of school. Sometimes disadvantaged students don't get recommended for the advanced classes that will prepare them well for college, but other times they remove themselves from consideration, fearing that they can't handle the work, that they will lose friends in the transition, or that their classroom lessons will ignore their cultural heritage (Viadero, 2002).

As principal, one of Emily Cole's toughest tasks at Davis was over-coming the legacy of low expectations, persuading everyone in the school community that poor children could succeed with the right preparation. Essentially, she had to create a college-prep program from scratch.

She quickly learned to ask for help. McLaughlin, for example, smoothed over some early conflicts between the faculties at the University of Houston–Downtown and Davis over the best way to run the summer college institute. The university representatives thought their job was to diagnose problems and prescribe solutions, McLaughlin said. They were not accustomed to collaborating with high school educators, figuring out how both sides could make changes to help more students earn college degrees. In addition, McLaughlin said, some university staff members immediately wanted to expel Davis students who misbehaved at the summer institute instead of showing them how to act on a college campus and giving them time to improve.

After 3 years of intervening between the college and the high school, McLaughlin paid for a professional mediator to sort through the problems. She also encouraged the university to provide office space on campus for Communities in Schools counselors who could work more closely with the Davis students. Eventually, the university and high school staffs worked out their differences and became very supportive of the summer institute. But "that love affair wasn't instant," McLaughlin said.

McLaughlin also taught Cole how to write successful grant applications, and she introduced her to wealthy benefactors who would commit money for special projects. The elected constable for the neighborhood, the local priest, and the staff at Communities in Schools proved ready sources of ideas for reaching out to merchants and getting parents and grandparents to buy into the new vision for the high school. Davis counselor Pat Notaro and scholarship coordinator Shanya Gensior held regular meetings for parents to talk about the college admissions process, course requirements, and financial aid.

None of the grand ambitions had a chance of succeeding without sub-stantial improvements in the classroom, however. And few people realized the extent of the troubles at Davis. Expanding the limited academic op-tions for bright students like Griselda Mani was part of the challenge, but so was making significant changes in the curriculum for students with less motivation and aptitude.

Cole started a course to help students prepare for the college entrance exams and added honors-level math and English classes. After they signed up for the college scholarship offer, students would pester the principal for help getting into the college-prep courses, but the teachers refused to admit anyone who hadn't taken the prerequisites.

"The teachers would say, 'You can't do this. You're not prepared. You can't pass this course,'" Cole recalled. "The kids would come running to me saying, 'Please, get me in that class. I need it to get my scholarship.' And I kept saying, 'Listen to your teacher. How are you going to do it?' So I would get a contract with them whereby they would have to get tutoring and do their homework."

At the same time that she was encouraging students to take challenging classes at Davis, Cole was making sure the teachers were capable of leading them. She hired some new instructors who supported her vision for the school and provided training for veterans.

"They were really supportive of new teachers at Davis," said Susan Miller, a Teach for America instructor who joined the staff in 1992 to teach math, science, and SAT prep after earning a degree from Cornell University. "But it was a hard year. It was the kind of thing where you never felt you could do enough. There were so many things you couldn't change. When a kid comes in and doesn't know multiplication tables, what do you do? That happened a lot. I would let the kids use calculators as a support so they wouldn't need to keep counting on their fingers."

Myron Greenfield, who joined the Davis faculty in 1989, said he encountered a "big cloud of negativity" from many veteran teachers. Don't assign a book report to his 9th-grade English classes, they told him, because the students don't read and won't turn in the assignment. Greenfield did it anyway and got almost universal compliance. Stick with basic texts, they said, because the students won't understand complex literature. Greenfield assigned Thoreau and Emerson and was stunned by the students' insights about transcendentalism.

"They told me not to teach [Orwell's] *1984*. They wouldn't 'get it,'" Greenfield said. "I have kids who have graduated who still mention *1984*, [*The Great*] *Gatsby*, *Their Eyes Were Watching God*, *The Scarlet Letter* . . . Kids are so much smarter than adults. They know which teachers have expectations for them, and they know which teachers are there to get the measly paycheck and get out by 3:30."

Greenfield's assessment is backed up by numerous studies of teachers' attitudes and performance. Only one fourth of secondary school students nationwide say they like their teachers and find their classes challenging (MetLife, Inc., 2001). The lowest rankings come from students in high-poverty schools. While three fourths of Latino and African-American students say they have high expectations for their futures, just 40% of the teachers in the high-poverty schools these students usually attend believe the teenagers will succeed.

At Davis, Cole and her administrative team toughened their tactics with burned-out teachers, counseling some of them to leave the profession and giving poor performance reviews to others, which reduced their pay raises. Among those receiving low ratings was the Davis representative to the Houston teacher's union.

Robert Stockwell, the school district's chief academic officer who was then the dean of instruction at Davis, said most of the veteran teachers on staff didn't believe that minority students could excel in school. They focused on the few eager students and "pretty much ignored the rest . . . The school thought of itself as a sorting system: These kids study and the rest of you just need to be able to read and vote."

Before Cole came to Davis, Stockwell had spent 2 years as the school's assistant principal. In that role, he said he frequently observed teachers and found that most lectured, from start to finish, in class.

"Sometimes they'd be standing there lecturing to themselves," he said. "The kids are asleep and are at the maximum possible distance from the teacher. It was like the teachers and kids were in two different worlds."

In addition to pressuring the poor performers, Davis administrators began providing regular professional development for the faculty to show them different ways to teach. But it was only the beginning of a serious shift in thinking about the goals that students and teachers were capable of achieving.

At the end of the 1992–93 school year, 93 Davis students had qualified for the Tenneco scholarships, representing 47% of the graduating class. Eighty students subsequently enrolled in college, four times the post-secondary attendance rate in 1989.

It was compelling, almost unbelievable progress. But in Jim Ketelsen's view, the news wasn't good enough. "When I looked at it, what we had done was take the top half of the kids who were probably going to graduate high school anyway and helped more of them go to college," he said. "The bottom half still dropped out, and we had no impact whatsoever on them."

Chapter 2

A FOUNDATION FOR THE FUTURE

One of the key lessons from Tenneco's early experience with Davis is that a college scholarship alone won't turn around the fortunes of disadvantaged students. Money is only part of the solution. Students fighting for a better future also need effective instruction and dedicated mentors who will challenge them academically and keep them emotionally close to their hearts.

Because the academic weaknesses of students in the Near North Side were so vast, Jim Ketelsen knew he couldn't provide everything they needed. But he believed he could reinforce the basics—reading, writing, and math—and give the students a realistic chance of succeeding in other subjects. He also wanted to improve discipline in the feeder system because teachers were spending so much time trying to restore order that they couldn't concentrate on instruction. For months, Ketelsen traveled around the country examining reading, math, and classroom-management programs, looking specifically for those that had demonstrated good results with poor and minority students.

After consulting with the founders of Success for All, MOVE IT Math, and Consistency Management & Cooperative Discipline®, and asking them to review each other's work for compatibility, Ketelsen contacted all the principals in the Davis feeder system. Because Houston is a right-to-work state, school district officials said they were required only to notify the teacher's union of the plan for the Davis feeder schools. Susan Sclafani, who was the district's director of curriculum at the time, said the major concern union leaders had was whether teachers would be paid for training. Project GRAD agreed to provide compensation, meals, and materials.

"Clearly, any district in which there is a collective bargaining agreement had to negotiate in a different manner than we did in Houston," Sclafani acknowledged. "It's a more difficult issue."

Ketelsen insisted that 75% of the teachers vote to approve each school's participation because he didn't want to put programs in place unless most of the faculty would agree to support them. After securing the necessary votes in six elementary schools, one middle school, and one high school, Ketelsen then searched for money to pay for the curricula and training. He quickly obtained a $10,000 donation from an individual benefactor and a $50,000 grant from the McNair Foundation of Houston. One by one, he pulled in contributions to pay for the programs' license fees, buy workbooks, and set up professional development sessions for teachers and principals. That first year, 60 teachers in the Davis feeder system attended the professional development sessions sponsored by the Ketelsens, 30 hours of instructional support for each person. The Ketelsens participated in all the sessions, showing up nearly every Saturday for weeks on end.

Although many teachers in the Davis feeder system appreciated the training and expressed gratitude for the catered lunches and comfortable meeting space, some demonstrated their displeasure by folding their arms across their chests and glaring at their hosts. To Kathryn Ketelsen, the hostile postures said, "Teach me if you can. I dare you."

Such negative reactions are fairly typical in the first years of education reform, said Dr. Kwame A. Opuni, a former HISD research specialist who now directs the Center for Research on School Reform at the University of St. Thomas in Houston. He has been evaluating the Davis High School changes since 1988 and the impact of Project GRAD since it started in 1993. Opuni said teachers in urban schools often feel besieged by factors outside their control and are isolated from other instructors in their buildings. They don't have many opportunities to observe innovative instruction or to participate in meaningful professional development. Many teachers in these settings work very hard, he said, but they don't necessarily know or use effective strategies in the classroom. When someone asks them to adopt new methods, they often resent the break in their routines, however ineffective their habits might be.

Some teachers in the Davis feeder system responded in a similar manner, Opuni said, particularly when they had to attend training sessions on Saturdays and implement all the Project GRAD components at once. The organizers learned from that experience and later phased in the training over time, he said, "so teachers don't get overwhelmed."

Instructional quality seemed to be the biggest variable at Davis in the early years of Project GRAD. Because most of Ketelsen's school reforms targeted the elementary grades, high school students experienced few changes at first. Cole and others continued trying to strengthen the curriculum at Davis, giving students a fair chance of succeeding in college through more challenging high school courses. But it took time to rebuild and retrain the staff. Many people in the Davis High School community— students, parents, and teachers—remained skeptical that the teenagers could succeed in college.

"Although Mr. Ketelsen and Mrs. Cole had started the Tenneco scholarships, the faculty really believed the kids could not do the job," said Kathryn Ekstrom, who joined the Davis staff in 1992 as dean of instruction. "They said, 'Sure, you can offer scholarships, but first they won't go, and if they do go, they won't make it.' When I first got there, there were probably 90 teachers and probably 20% believed that [all] kids could learn."

Ekstrom quickly observed that the biggest impediment to improving instruction was the limited way in which most of the Davis faculty taught: They lectured. They relied on textbooks, rarely leading students to primary source materials. They passed out worksheets, which required a simple recall of facts, instead of applying knowledge through writing, analyzing, demonstrating, or performing. When Ekstrom discussed alternative in-structional approaches, most of the teachers stared at her, uncomprehending. They had never experienced anything different.

The teaching practices at Davis were hardly unique. Martin Haberman, a professor of curriculum and instruction at the University of Wisconsin–Milwaukee, refers to the limited instructional repertoire common in urban schools as "the pedagogy of poverty" because it assumes poor children are incapable of handling complexity, applying information, using technology, and investing in their education (Haberman, 1991). He said many teachers in urban schools use a basic classroom menu that includes giving directions, monitoring seatwork, reading while students listen, settling disputes, marking papers, and giving grades. Such techniques encourage passivity in students and characterize the low expectations teachers have for them. Moreover, these kind of instructional practices reward obedience and memorization instead of encouraging students to develop personal responsibility and analytical thinking skills that are vital for success in college.

"Unfortunately, the pedagogy of poverty does not work," Haberman writes. "Youngsters achieve neither minimum levels of life skills nor what they are capable of learning. The classroom atmosphere created by constant teacher direction and student compliance seethes with passive resentment that sometimes bubbles up into overt resistance. Teachers burn out because of the emotional and physical energy that they must expend to maintain their authority every hour of every day.

"The pedagogy of poverty requires that teachers who begin their careers intending to be helpers, models, guides, stimulators, and caring sources of encouragement transform themselves into directive authoritarians in order to function in urban schools. But people who choose to become teachers do not do so because at some point they decided, 'I want to be able to tell people what to do all day and then make them do it!' This gap between expectations and reality means that there is a pervasive, fundamental, irreconcilable difference between the motivation of those who select themselves to become teachers and the demands of urban teaching" (Haberman, 1991, pp. 291–292).

Somehow, Project GRAD had to find a way to change the picture.

ORGANIZING FOR LONG-TERM SUCCESS

The Ford Foundation, with $11.3 billion in assets, is the third largest philanthropic organization in the United States (Wilhelm, 2002). Its massive office building, which fills almost an entire block on East 43rd Street in New York City, attests to the foundation's extensive reach supporting non-profit groups around the world. Founded in 1936 with gifts and bequests of Ford Motor Company stock by Henry and Edsel Ford, the foundation has made available more than $10 billion in grants and loans, although it no longer owns Ford stock.

Normally, when the Ford Foundation considers funding requests, program officials review the submitted proposals to see if they fit the philanthropy's objectives. Then they determine if the applicants have evidence of strong organizational controls and a reasonable chance of success. Members of the foundation's Board of Trustees set broad policy for the organization and, occasionally, they might pass on tips about worthy endeavors. But, generally, they let the foundation's staff choose the projects to finance.

That's not the path Project GRAD followed, however. Steven Zwerling, Ford's senior director of the Education, Media, Arts, and Culture Department, first heard about the Houston school reforms in 1994 during a quarterly meeting of the foundation's Board of Trustees. Members of the foundation's board who knew Ketelsen through their mutual corporate and philanthropic connections had listened to him describe, in the most passionate terms, Tenneco's efforts to resurrect Davis High School.

At their behest, Zwerling "reluctantly" went to Houston to take a look at the changes occurring in the Davis feeder system. From what he knew about the program, Zwerling didn't think Project GRAD would fit within Ford's grant-making priorities, which included funding independent evaluations of education reform initiatives but rarely the initiatives themselves. He was also aware of many competing education reform models around the country, and he worried that if Ford started choosing among them, it would set off an intense competition for financial support.

Nevertheless, Zwerling and two other Ford associates with experience in education traveled to Houston to see Project GRAD in action. They visited classrooms, talked to teachers and principals, and reviewed the supporting data. Although they were impressed with the results, they were still reluctant to approve a grant from Ford. One hesitation was that Project GRAD seemed to be synonymous with Ketelsen and, perhaps, limited to his direct involvement. Students and teachers affectionately referred to the tall, white-haired man as "the big guy" or "the white man," a compassionate person who thought more disadvantaged kids should be able to go to college.

"We were wondering about the Ketelsen effect, almost as if they were trying to 'win one for the Gipper,'" Zwerling said. To make sure that educators weren't dazzling him with their success stories and hiding their flaws, Zwerling returned to Houston for an extended visit, this time without tour guides. During his informal walks through the hallways, teachers beckoned him to visit their classrooms. He also randomly selected students and asked for their impressions of the changes occurring in their schools.

"From seeing the little ones doing pre-algebra and hearing juniors and seniors say, 'I'm not getting pregnant. I'm going to college,' there was the whole spectrum," Zwerling said. "In addition to that and [higher] test scores and graduation rates, there was no doubt that after my third trip, there was something special going on in this feeder."

The cosmetic changes were backed by statistics gathered by Kwame Opuni. Besides documenting improvements in test scores, attendance, and graduation rates, Opuni had attended the Project GRAD training sessions so he would understand how the various program components should be implemented. Every year, he also surveyed teachers to gauge their opinions of the reforms. Had their relations with students improved? Were administrators supporting the changes? Did they have fewer discipline problems and, if so, how much time had they saved for instruction? Opuni looked for trends, then compared the findings with earlier benchmarks. In 1998, Opuni noted that new teachers gave high ratings to the training and support that Project GRAD provided for the three major curricular components, with no area receiving less than 75% satisfaction. Veteran teachers were slightly less enthusiastic (Opuni, 1999).

James LaVois, who was then an assistant superintendent with authority over schools in the Davis feeder system, previously served as the principal of another high school in Houston. He said he had envied the resources and success of the Project GRAD schools and wished his school could join them. When he became an assistant superintendent, he supported Project GRAD by removing two principals who had not helped teachers implement the program.

"If those two schools had had success, then it would have been fine. The degree of their implementation wouldn't have mattered," said LaVois, who is now assistant superintendent for school support services and athletics. "But they did not have success. So therefore, I had to get different leadership. You fight your best battle because there are always those that resist. What you hope is that you can find the right mix with the right people. And the ones that aren't the right mix move on."

The turnover of principals and teachers in the Davis feeder system remained fairly high—and mostly voluntary—after schools joined Project GRAD. Of the nine original principals, for example, only one was still working in the cluster a decade later. Sherman Elementary School endured four principal changes and Marshall Middle School went through three. Each time a new administrator or teacher started working in the Davis cluster, Project GRAD provided him or her with orientation and training. The continual shuffling of educators and students is one of the few constants in urban schools, and Project GRAD had to deal with that reality. What made the Davis High School feeder system different from those in other urban communities was the continuation of nearly identical curricular programs that the schools used. The Davis schools weren't switching instructional models every few years, as many urban schools do. For the most part, educators knew what they were getting into when they came to the Near North Side of Houston, so their classrooms became more consistent over time.

Meanwhile, at the Ford Foundation, Zwerling was ready to recommend that the organization invest in Project GRAD. He believed that Ketelsen had taken the right approach in Houston by focusing on a cluster of schools instead of limiting his reach to a single school, where the changes might not survive the absence of a group of dedicated educators. Ketelsen also had attained a certain economy of scale by working with about 6,000 students. Their achievements were becoming so widespread that they couldn't be dismissed as a fluke.

At the same time, Zwerling didn't think Project GRAD would be recognized as an unqualified success until it could be exported. People had to be sure that the improvements weren't just due to the particular demographics of the Davis feeder system or to Ketelsen's leadership. He recommended that Ketelsen expand Project GRAD to a second cluster of schools in Houston and get another city to adopt the program, too. Zwerling told Ketelsen that the foundation could "provide some funds to support the ongoing efforts in the first feeder, funds to help you expand into subsequent feeders in Houston, but as a national funder the only way we can justify funding a local project is to also find out if it can be replicated in other places."

Nevertheless, he cautioned Ketelsen not to be seduced by the grant. Sometimes organizations change directions and missions to gain access to an enticing money stream, he said, instead of making good choices for the long-term health of their programs.

Ford's conditions were not unusual in the world of philanthropy. Increasingly, foundations are issuing stronger directives to the non-profit organizations they support in order to encourage better returns on their investments, said Bill Porter, executive director of the association Grantmakers for Education. Porter also said the hands-on involvement and technical assistance provided by foundations mark the difference between ordinary charitable contributions and philanthropy, which uses money to address broad social problems.

In 1996, Ketelsen accepted Ford's donation—and its terms and conditions—on behalf of Project GRAD. During the 1996–97 school year, Project GRAD started working with a second feeder system in Houston. This one included 15 schools serving about 9,000 predominately African-American students who matriculated at Jack Yates High School, located in an area of Houston known as the Third Ward. The student population in the Yates cluster differed from the one served by Davis High School, which gave Project GRAD an opportunity to test its methods in a diverse environment.

However, there was one significant problem at the start. The college scholarship offer was so alluring that many teachers and administrators—particularly at the high school level—believed that signing on with Project GRAD meant nothing more than getting financial assistance for students. They were not prepared to change their approach to teaching disadvantaged youths. Getting people to accept the dual function of Project GRAD—to provide more opportunities in exchange for accepting greater responsibilities—became one of the most perplexing problems of the reform model's expansion beyond Davis High School.

Chapter 3

ACADEMIC SUPPORT FOR COLLEGE

Sandy Lopez wasn't focused on college when a smuggler, who was supposed to take him from Honduras to Houston, left him alone in a Mexican desert at the age of 15. Nor was he focused on college when he flunked the first semester of 9th grade at Davis High School in 1992. "I was just going to go to school until I was 18 and then start working and help the family," Sandy said.

Struggling to learn a new language and battling bullies at school, Sandy joined the Davis ROTC program where his teachers gave him a spiffy uniform, taught him self-discipline, and challenged him to speak English. They also expected him to perform public service. One of his first assignments was to participate in the school's annual Walk for Success, where educators and community volunteers visit students' homes and explain the Project GRAD scholarship requirements to their families. In preparing for the event, Sandy met Shanya Gensior, Project GRAD's scholarship coordinator at Davis, who encouraged him to get involved in school activities and start planning his future. "If I hadn't graduated," he said, "I would have disappointed her so much."

In 1993 and 1994, Sandy also participated in Project GRAD's 4-week summer institute at the University of Houston–Downtown. An open-enrollment commuter college whose campus is so close to Davis that students disparagingly refer to it as "13th grade," the university nevertheless felt like another world to Sandy. "I remember we used to sit in the middle of the hall, my friends and I, or we'd just walk around the building and pretend that we were college students," he said. "That was the moment when we realized, 'Hey, this could happen.'"

In 1995, Sandy's horizons widened when he and five other students from Davis attended a 6-week summer institute at Cornell University. Although he thought the biggest challenge would be surviving his first airplane ride, Sandy found greater obstacles on campus. On the first day of classes he discovered that he would have to write a substantial research paper each week for his English course and prepare two major speeches for his communications course. One evening, with a half-finished paper due the next day and no computer of his own to use, he hiked several miles to an all-night computer lab and stayed there through the morning completing the assignment.

"Believe me, I was feeling very crappy after my first week of classes because I didn't know how to write a paper," he said. "This is what my English teacher told me: 'You don't know how to write a paper. We don't write papers like this.' She was forgiving because we were high school students, but she told me, 'You need to buy this book. Write papers like this book says.' It's called *Writing College Essays*. I still have it. She told me very frankly, 'High school is different.'"

Davis students began attending the Cornell University Summer College program in 1993 through the intervention of Susan Miller, one of three young instructors who had joined the faculty from the Teach for America program. Since 1989, the national teaching corps has placed more than 8,000 recent college graduates—many of them from elite universities—in urban and rural public schools where they agree to stay for least 2 years.

Although Miller was impressed that the Tenneco scholarship offer had boosted Davis's college attendance rate, she became concerned when many students did not earn degrees. Sometimes the students dropped out to support their families, but Miller believed many failed to thrive because they couldn't break out of the depressed neighborhoods they returned home to each night. Research confirms the tendency of Latino students nationally to attend 2-year commuter colleges where they typically maintain only part-time status. This significantly reduces their chances of earning a degree (Fry, 2002).

The goal of the Cornell program, Miller said, was "to give kids a college experience so they would know what it was like to go away."

Miller had graduated from Cornell and knew about its selective summer program for high school students. About 3,600 students from around the country participate each year, taking regular college courses alongside students who have already been admitted to Cornell. The application process is similar to the regular college admissions process, but the bigger barrier for some students is the cost—$4,100 per student in 1993, $6,565 each by 2003.

The Tenneco Foundation provided a full scholarship for one Davis student to attend the first summer institute at Cornell, Kraft Foods provided another, and the Cornell alumni association in Houston paid the fees for two more. Cornell agreed to provide a full scholarship for every four students who attended from Davis. Students and teachers raised additional funds from local businesses and from car washes and bake sales.

Working with Gensior, the Davis faculty chose seven juniors to attend the Cornell summer program in the summer of 1993. They were not necessarily the top students, Miller said, but had made significant academic progress, which their teachers wanted to honor. One student was homeless. Another was in an abusive relationship.

Miller took the students to Ithaca, New York and stayed on Cornell's campus that summer so she would be nearby if they had trouble. Each of the teenagers signed up for two courses during the summer session. All of them struggled because their academic preparation was weaker than what most of their Cornell classmates had received.

"But it wasn't disastrous," Miller said. "They got [college] credit. They worked very hard." And the students said the Cornell experience "made a difference their senior year" of high school. "They would talk all the time about 'what I learned at Cornell.'"

Ten juniors from Davis went to Cornell the next summer, with Miller shouldering the fund-raising and logistical work. The new Cornell group included a mix of high-achieving students and some motivated students whose grades were above average. Miller found teachers to mentor the students before and after the summer program.

In addition to taking English composition and a course of their choosing at Cornell, the 1994 group participated in a career exploration seminar to help them understand the preparation they would need to succeed in higher education. The Davis students started a college club when they returned to Houston so they could share their experiences with other students.

After his summer at Cornell, Sandy Lopez came back feeling "cocky" about his new skills and impatient for high school to end. In addition to his regular high school load, he took two courses at the University of Houston–Downtown during his senior year and, with the two classes he completed at Cornell, he accumulated a total of 12 hours of college credit by the time he graduated from high school. Despite posting a composite SAT score of only 800 out of a possible 1,600 points, he was admitted to Cornell and received a $50,000 scholarship. Altogether, he said he received 10 scholarship offers worth a total of $140,000.

Sandy left the Ivy League after just one semester, however. He had never lived outside a tropical climate and the frigid temperatures in New York State gave him a persistent cold and a depressed spirit. Because he only had enough money to pay for a return plane ticket at the end of the school year, he spent a lonely Thanksgiving holiday on campus eating pizza with three international students who also didn't have anywhere else to go.

"That was the saddest day," he said. "I remember I went to my dorm and cried. I didn't want to come back. I had a terrible, terrible time."

Sandy transferred to Texas Lutheran University, where he activated another scholarship offer. He thrived in the new environment and earned a bachelor's degree in psychology. By transferring some credits to the University of Houston–Downtown and taking classes there when his mother became ill, he was able to obtain a second bachelor's degree in communications. He now works as a scholarship coordinator at Sam Houston High School, passing on his hard-earned advice to other Project GRAD scholars.

"YOU NEED TO KNOW THAT YOU'RE NOT STUPID"

Establishing the belief by encouraging disadvantaged students to attend college is the first step. Providing an incentive by offering a college scholarship is the second step. Developing their skills by steering them into college preparatory classes is the third step. But the fourth step—supporting students emotionally and academically by sending them to college during their summer vacations—might be the strongest inducement of all. Being on a college campus, learning with and from college students, understanding the expectations of college professors—these are the experiences that build awareness of what it takes to succeed. Gustavo Rivera, a 1998 graduate of Davis High School, said, "I think those summer programs were not only necessary but they made me ready for college. They were the wrapping paper around the education."

The summer institute, which preceded the formation of Project GRAD, has remained an integral part of the reform initiative because it acts as a bridge for students who are navigating the unfamiliar path to college. Students who sign up for Project GRAD take much of the program's promises on faith, but to fully embrace the idea that they can compete with other college-bound students they need tangible evidence that they belong. Through the summer institute, Project GRAD gives students the opportunity to see their educational goals up close.

That's not an unimportant vision. Disadvantaged teenagers often require experiential identification with a successful future to fight against images pulling them in the opposite direction. On one side, they can see the apparently easy lives of high school dropouts who no longer have to tote textbooks or study for tests. The dead-end jobs that dropouts can secure right out of school seem promising to students whose families often depend on multiple minimum-wage paychecks. On the other side, they see professionals who have to spend 4, 6, or 8 years in school beyond the 12th grade before they attain a noticeable increase in pay and prestige.

In many urban school districts, teenagers choose the dropout route more frequently than the path to college. Just 52% of the students who started high school in Houston during the 1990s graduated 4 years later, according to one study, and the completion rate for Latino students was even more dismal—only 42% stayed through the 12th grade (Greene, 2002). Nationally the percentage of young Latino adults who had earned high school diplomas by age 29 rose from 48% in 1972 to 63% by 2000, but that figure was still well below the rates for young white adults—93%—and young black adults—85%. African-American students comprise 17% of public school enrollments and 13% of college populations, while Latinos make up 16% and 9% of those populations, respectively. But African-Americans and Latinos earn just 9% and 6% of all bachelor's degrees awarded in the United States (Noeth & Wimberly, n.d.).

A major study of the differences between students' aspirations for college and their completion rates found that disadvantaged students tend to receive limited and incorrect advice about higher education. Many students believe that completing minimal high school graduation requirements is the only preparation they need for college, regardless of the quality of the courses they passed. Fewer than 12% understand the admissions criteria for either selective or accessible colleges (Venezia, Kirst, & Antonio, n.d.).

A study by the Pew Hispanic Center found that while more than 80% of Latino high school graduates go to college by age 26—about the same rate as white high school graduates do—only 23% of Latino high school graduates earn a bachelor's degree, which is less than half the rate of white students, and 64% fail to earn any post-secondary credential (Fry, 2004). As the report noted: "Thus, the disparity between white and Latino college students in finishing a bachelor's degree is larger than the high school completion gap and is the largest attainment gap facing Hispanic youth as they progress through the U.S. education system" (pp. 2–3).

Before he enrolled in Project GRAD, Gustavo Rivera said he knew very little about the skills and courses that would prepare him for college. Like Sandy Lopez, he credits the summer institutes for laying the foundation for his future. Gustavo's first exposure to college occurred in 1995, the summer after his freshman year at Davis High School, when he took a biology prep course at the Jesse H. Jones Academic Institute at the University of Houston–Downtown. "I loved that course," he said. "We got to dissect a cat and had all these field trips."

Gustavo participated in the University of Houston–Downtown's summer institute for 2 years, taking classes during the first half of the summer and pursuing a paid internship during the second half. His job—developing health awareness programs for young people—took him to the University of Texas School of Public Health at the Houston Medical Center, where he also shadowed professionals on the job. Working for a program called Safer Choices, he researched sexually transmitted diseases and performed educational skits about them on the radio and before community groups. During the second summer, he also mentored first-year students in the program.

"I'm very grateful for these summer institutes," Gustavo said. "First of all, it placed us in a college ambiance with real-life college students. You're not living the college life but you're introduced to a college campus when you're fourteen years old. That prepares you academically and socially.

"Of course, these people I met, my bosses, I'll never forget. They were awesome. They gave me my first job and my first paycheck. They gave me

experience in the field I wanted to go into. It was an unimaginable opportunity for a kid like me. For inner-city kids, all the parents, contacts, and
relations, they're mechanics and painters, hard-working people, but still
not professional. You don't know exactly what a dentist does or what kind
of a lifestyle a lawyer maintains. It's pretty distant. Things are vague until
you connect with someone who has that dream of yours."

Gustavo thought he would become a physician, but his junior year
chemistry class at Davis High School turned him away from a medical
career. A substitute teacher presided for the first half of the one-semester
chemistry course (on the school's extended block schedule model). Gustavo
said he learned next to nothing in this essential prerequisite for a career in
medicine. He called chemistry "the worst class of my life" because the
temporary teacher's instruction was limited to giving students a copy of
the Periodic Table of Elements to memorize.

After his junior year, however, Gustavo secured one of the coveted
spots in the Cornell summer program. This "life-changing" summer at an
Ivy League university introduced him to the upper echelon of academic
life and showed him he belonged. But first, he had to get through English
composition. He earned an F on his first writing assignment at Cornell.
Demoralized but not defeated, he started meeting with a teaching assistant after every class to find out how he could improve his skills. His
older brother and sister urged him during long-distance telephone calls
not to get discouraged. They told him that as a bilingual student whose
elementary-educated parents had emigrated from Mexico, he couldn't be
expected to sail through a college English course. But that didn't mean
he couldn't pass the class. "You need to know that you're not stupid,"
they told him.

At the end of the 6-week summer session, Gustavo not only raised his
English grade up from an F to an A-, he also figured out the combination of
initiative, effort, resourcefulness, and scholarship that lead to achievement
at a top university.

"I needed to reread my work and edit and get somebody to read behind
me," he said, laying out the lessons he gained about writing college papers.
"It's not just about writing [it one time], but about the final product. Just
read it out loud so you can hear what's wrong with it. It's better to say it in
three sentences than in one long, incomprehensible sentence."

After the Cornell institute, Gustavo returned to Davis High School invigorated and illuminated. The five other students who had attended the same summer program became his best friends at school, he said, and all six went to the senior prom together. The summer institute helped them shift their sights beyond high school as well. Of the six, he said that all but one graduated from college in 4 years; the one nongraduate is just a few credits shy of a degree.

Gustavo took the advice of a mentor at Cornell who told him that top universities were eager to recruit motivated, high-achieving Latino students and would provide substantial financial aid to help them. He subsequently earned scholarships to Cornell, Georgetown University, Macalester College, Princeton University, the University of Texas, and the University of Virginia. Although his heart was with Cornell because of his positive summer experience there, he chose Princeton because the school offered him the most money.

It was the right decision, he says, looking back. But there were times when he doubted his choice and his abilities. When he struggled at Princeton, he remembered Ruth Kravatz's math classes at Davis High School, where he earned a few F's but eventually passed both pre-calculus and calculus, despite being "horrible at math." Gustavo said he even joined Kravatz's Mental Math team in his senior year (though he frequently lost matches to freshmen and sophomores) because she "motivated me so much" and was so approachable: "She said, 'Gustavo, I know you hate math, but I have this friend who went to Princeton'—and this is before I considered going there—'and he's a lawyer and he said the class that helped him most in life was calculus because it helped him systematically with the law. Even if you never see calculus again, you'll be glad you took it.'"

When he struggled with his writing in college, Gustavo remembered how Davis English teacher Myron Greenfield told him that he had "a voice and an ability to move words, but you need to expand your vocabulary and write more." A writer writes, Greenfield told him, so Gustavo kept practicing.

"He would say, 'I don't care if you are a Latino . . . I don't care if you are poor or living under a bridge, in my class you will succeed,'" Gustavo recalled: "That was such an important message. It's like you wear a cross, a burden of being an inner-city kid, of not being white. You see the police, the society as your enemy because you are attacking it or coming from the outside. You figure you don't belong. Your parents are immigrants. Your brother might be in jail and your sister is pregnant. You feel like you have to pull a lot to get anywhere. You have to drag that cross. When you undo it and say, 'At least for this hour and a half, that will not exist.' When you are a student in Mr. Greenfield's class, that shouldn't affect you at all."

In 2002 Gustavo earned a bachelor's degree in anthropology from Princeton. He plans to attend graduate school and pursue a career as a documentary filmmaker.

"In my life I had teachers who not only taught but worried about the other aspects of my life—both hands and heart," he said. "Maybe some day these summer institutes won't be necessary because of the high level of achievement at Davis."

TRAINING STUDENTS TO COMPETE

The summer college institute is not unique to Project GRAD. Many universities sponsor summer preparatory sessions for high school students, although most of the spots go to teenagers whose parents can afford the steep fees. College-preparatory programs aimed at disadvantaged populations, such as Upward Bound and A Better Chance, can help level the playing field but they don't reach all the students who need assistance (Noeth & Wimberly, n.d.).

A recent study of state-sponsored "early intervention" programs for disadvantaged students found a wide variation in their methods and impact (Cunningham, Redmond, & Merisotis, 2003). The study, which did not evaluate the Project GRAD summer institutes, determined that ongoing contact between the staff and the participants was essential to their success, as were coordinated efforts between universities and high schools. However, the greatest challenge for the programs was deciding whether to emphasize quality or quantity. The more extensive the services offered, the more likely students will succeed. But the higher costs associated with a more multifaceted approach means that fewer students can be helped overall.

The Jesse H. Jones Academic Institute at the University of Houston–Downtown started with 200 students from Davis High School but has grown to 350–400 students each summer more than a decade later. From the beginning, the institute's organizers tried to create a serious college-preparatory program instead of a "feel-good summer camp," said coordinator Branden Kuzmick. Davis students ride school buses to and from the campus each day and attend most classes with their peers, but they are encouraged to interact with college students on campus. The high school students can also earn $150 summer stipends only by demonstrating good attendance during the half-day sessions and by completing their assignments. (Students who qualify for the institute's science program, which emphasizes math as a tool for inquiry in biology, chemistry, and physics, attend extended-day sessions that include enrichment classes, labs, and field trips.)

The summer institute faculty seeks to motivate students by creating thematic units that will appeal to teenagers and by making contemporary connections to reading, writing, and math lessons. For example, the 2002 curriculum centered on law enforcement. Students took field trips to state and district courts, the county jail, and the city morgue, and heard on-campus presentations from experts in forensics and criminal justice. In other years, the institute focused on topics such as terrorism, cloning, architecture, presidential elections, and weather changes.

Interest in the thematic approach inspired the University of Houston–Downtown faculty to develop additional interdisciplinary courses that students can take when they enroll there after high school. To further support the Project GRAD students when they come to the university after high school, faculty members set up a program called the Learners Community, which gives first-time college students access to advisers who can help them with course registration, counseling, study skills, and immigration snafus. Robin Davidson, director of the Learners Community, said the university created the 5-year pilot program in 2000 because many Davis graduates had a difficult time maintaining a C average in college and earning 24 credit hours per year to keep their scholarships.

"I would say Project GRAD has been very successful in getting students at Davis to graduate from high school," Davidson said. "But graduating from high school and succeeding in college are two different things."

Using a combination of federal and foundation grants, the university designed the Learners Community for freshmen and sophomores and will evaluate its impact on the students' academic performance over time. In the fall of 2002, the Learners Community enrolled 249 students, about half of them from Project GRAD schools and half randomly selected for participation.

One feature of the Learners Community program is the involvement of college juniors and seniors who serve as tutors and mentors. The upperclassmen receive stipends to attend classes with the Learners Community participants and meet with them afterward to discuss the major topics, giving students opportunities to ask questions they might be afraid to mention to professors.

"First-generation college students, which is different from first-time college students, absolutely do not have the models for what higher education culture is," Davidson said. "So, we're working on that with them, trying to help them understand what it is to be part of a university, what kind of study skills are involved, the fact that you have to re-enroll each semester, that you don't just continue on like in high school. These are very basic things, but how would they know?"

Project GRAD affiliates in Houston and other cities have tried a range of strategies over the years to strengthen the summer institutes. In Los Angeles, for example, a year-round school schedule designed to ease overcrowding causes some students to attend classes during the summer months, which prevents them from attending the required summer college institutes. Setting up alternative institutes that meet during the regular school year is possible, but also more costly and cumbersome because colleges are in session then, space on campus is at a premium, professors who provide most of the instruction are busy teaching their regular course loads, and college students who act as assistants and mentors during the institutes are not available.

With help from a local community group called Pacoima Beautiful, Project GRAD–Los Angeles subsequently designed a separate college institute that runs for 4 weeks in March and April. Integrating scientific research with service learning, the program enables high school students to design projects that will benefit the neighborhoods in which they live. Students meet with college professors and specialists in the field. During one session, a group of students monitored air quality in the area. Another group brought public officials and neighborhood organizations together to discuss environmental problems associated with commercial development near a local dam. The following year, another group of students attending the alternative college institute designed a project based on the recommendations from the first group's dam study.

In Houston, the summer college institute options have evolved as well. As greater numbers of Davis High School students enrolled in advanced courses and applied to selective universities, the basic courses offered at the University of Houston–Downtown's summer institute weren't rigorous enough to challenge them. In 2000, Rice University established a Summer Mathematics Academy for Project GRAD students who are at the top of their high school classes and aspire to selective universities. The new program is open to qualified students from any of the Houston Project GRAD schools.

The partnership with Project GRAD gives Rice the chance to strengthen the academic preparation of minority students so more of them can compete at top universities. Gaining familiarity with the Rice campus also might encourage greater numbers of qualified minority students to seek admission to Rice after high school, which in turn would help the university reach its diversity goals.

Eighty-two sophomores, juniors, and seniors from Davis, Yates, Wheatley, and Reagan high schools attended Rice in the summer of 2002. Each student had a grade-point average of 3.5 or higher on a 4.0 scale. Most of the students had taken Advanced Placement courses as well. During the summer session, the teenagers take algebra II, pre-calculus, or calculus classes 3 hours a day for 4 weeks to prepare them for high-level math classes when they return to high school.

"What's exciting is that these students are on target or ahead of target" for completing a rigorous, college-preparatory math sequence that will "put them on a level playing field" with top students around the country, said Sharon L. Bush, project manager of the Rice Summer Mathematics Academy. "And we have four students in the calculus class who will be juniors," which means they will be ready for college-level calculus or differential equations courses during their senior year of high school.

In addition to setting up the summer academy, Rice formed a partnership with Technology for All, a non-profit group based in Houston, to provide a free personal computer and graphing calculator for each participant. The equipment, worth about $1,500 per set, gives the Project GRAD students the same tools that teenagers from higher-income families use routinely in advanced math and science courses. The computers also enable the Project GRAD students to research scholarships on the Internet and write essays for college admissions.

Teachers from the Houston Independent School District lead the summer institute classes. Rice chooses them based on the depth of their subject knowledge and their demonstrated skill conveying those concepts to teenagers. Only one of the teachers on the academy faculty during the summer of 2002 worked for a Project GRAD school.

Anne Papakonstantinou, director of an educational outreach program at Rice that has trained more than 4,000 Houston math teachers, said she tries to recruit top teachers from the same schools that the Project GRAD students attend. But most are not "of the caliber we would want." Papakonstantinou said Rice is working with Project GRAD to strengthen the training of high school math teachers so they can serve the students who are coming through the feeder system better prepared than previous classes.

Overall, the skills of Project GRAD students improve every year, said Linda Lewis, a regular teacher at the Rice Summer Mathematics Academy. But she sees clear differences among the academic standards at the participating schools, perhaps based on the length of time they have been part of Project GRAD and the level of commitment from the faculty and administration. In 2001, for example, the students from Davis High School "were very strong" and it was difficult to keep them engaged while getting the other students caught up. By contrast, the students from Yates High School, her alma mater, were not very advanced. And with regard to the students from Wheatley High School, Lewis said, "I couldn't tell if they were weak or strong. They're not motivated." The valedictorian from Wheatley that year was a brilliant mathematician, Lewis said, but his classmates "pulled him down" because they were not serious about learning. (Students from Reagan High School attended the Rice summer institute for the first time in 2002.)

Those impressions are supported by statistical evidence of changes in the students' math preparation. In 1996, only 49% of Davis High School graduates had passed algebra II (Opuni & Ochoa, 2002b). By 2000, 95%

had. Students at Yates and Wheatley have made slower gains completing algebra II, rising from 73% to 80% and 36% to 60% of the graduates, respectively, during the same period.

The level of support for the summer college sessions also varies from school to school. Administrators at three of the four schools provided bus transportation for students during the 2002 summer term at Rice, but students from Yates had to get to the campus on their own. Administrators at Rice believe that some high school staffs see the summer institute as a crucial link in the integrated system of support for high achievement, while others view the summer session as just another program they have to accommodate in a busy schedule. "Critical mass," Sharon Bush said diplomatically. "That's what they're really seeking in [Project] GRAD."

Chapter 4

SETTING UP THE SAFETY NET

It's difficult to know what will motivate students to stay in school, to return to school after dropping out, or to be more focused while they're in class. It's difficult to know which messages—positive or negative—a student will remember from all those uttered on a given day. And who should deliver the messages? How many times? In how many ways?

Teenagers tend to have myopic vision about the future. They want the instant gratification that American society conditions them to expect. The challenge is helping young people, particularly those who don't see much evidence of professional success in their normal surroundings, to develop a long-range perspective.

Children growing up in poor communities can't count on coming into contact with adults who will consistently keep their future in mind until they can confidently stand on their own. That's why Project GRAD tries to surround children with positive role models, including volunteer mentors, well-trained teachers, social workers, and parent advocates.

Communities in Schools (CIS) serves as the conduit for strengthening adult-child relationships in Project GRAD schools, but CIS could never rescue all the needy students single-handedly. Instead, the organization tries to create a system of support, drawing together all the people who have contact with children—parents, teachers, ministers, community workers, and committed volunteers—into the web of influence.

Cynthia Clay Briggs, executive director of Communities in Schools Houston, uses the expression, "how the ox got in the ditch" to explain why Jim Ketelsen added a social services component to Project GRAD. He understood, Briggs said, that teachers and principals have a difficult time putting children on the road to success if they don't know all the factors that caused them to fall off in the first place. People often complain when poor families receive special assistance from tax-supported social service agencies, she said, but they don't stop to think about how well-educated and connected families benefit from favorable tax laws, business and social networks, expert medical care, and other advantages of birth.

"So, what's different about an 11th grader at Davis High School having a Communities in Schools person pick up the phone and say, 'This child needs help'? " Briggs asked. "Why would one kid need less than others to be successful?"

Communities in Schools started in Houston in 1979 through the efforts of former District Judge Wyatt H. Heard, who was concerned that without appropriate intervention, the increasing numbers of alienated adolescents he saw in the juvenile justice system were destined for a life of crime. The model he brought back to Houston originated as Cities in Schools in Atlanta in the early 1960s. The organization's founder, Bill Milliken, set up "storefront academies" for poor urban youths who had dropped out of school and brought private and governmental support to the settings so the students would have access to career awareness, mentoring, and counseling, among other services. Today, Cities in Schools is the nation's largest stay-in-school network (Coalition for Juvenile Justice, 2001).

Houston left the national organization in 1986 and changed its name to Communities in Schools (CIS) Houston, a nonprofit agency that builds partnerships with public and private donors to serve children considered at risk of dropping out of school. CIS joined the Project GRAD network during the 1994–95 school year.

Project GRAD places at least one CIS social worker in each elementary school and teams of two to four social workers in each middle and high school. In addition to planning the annual Walk for Success event, CIS staff members coordinate tutoring and mentoring programs, provide counseling and referrals for problems such as truancy and substance abuse, and develop programs to show parents how to help their children succeed in school. CIS also recruits and trains parents for public speaking and leadership positions and invites some to serve on the Parent University Board of Trustees.

CIS asks parents to assist with the work of improving schools because the organization understands that educational change will not endure without the cooperation and support of families. Research supports this view. A study by the Cross City Campaign for Urban School Reform found that "organized parents and community members are essential to the reform process" and that "when school reform goes hand-in-hand with building strong communities, the institution of schooling itself changes fundamentally, increasing the chances that reform efforts will be carried out and sustained" (Gold, Simon, & Brown, 2002).

William Rios, Project GRAD–Houston's director of parent and community relations, recalled the first parent workshop he conducted at Sherman Elementary School in the Davis feeder system. The session focused on effective strategies that parents could use with their preschoolers at home. When the 30 mothers who attended said they thought their husbands should hear the same messages, Rios challenged them to lead a recruitment effort. At the next workshop 2 months later, Project GRAD provided babysitting services and teachers agreed to serve food. Because of the organizing efforts of the first group of mothers, the second session attracted 150 people, both men and women.

To Rios, the episode goes to the heart of community organizing in urban schools: "If anybody tries to do this by themselves, they'll either get burned out or not be successful. They need to find other people to work with them."

About 6,000 people a year attend the various Parent University programs offered in Houston through Project GRAD and CIS. Over the years, parents have mobilized to fight the county's plan to close a mental health clinic in an elementary school, persuaded city officials to raid the home of a drug dealer operating near a neighborhood school, and encouraged dozens of adults to take public speaking and high school equivalency courses.

In 2002, more than 1,000 Houston parents showed up for a public appreciation dinner sponsored by CIS. Theresia Spearman was among them. A mother of three, she said she was marginally involved in her children's schools before her doctors recommended that she be placed on full medical disability because of pulmonary hypertension. Accustomed to being busy, she decided to volunteer at nearby Foster Elementary School, whose 670 African-American students come primarily from two public housing projects wedged between the University of Houston and Texas Southern University. Foster is part of the Jack Yates High School feeder system, the second to join Project GRAD.

Spearman started answering telephones at Foster. Later she agreed to serve as president of the school's PTA and direct other volunteer functions. It was through CIS, however, that she learned how to turn her involvement into activism. Robert Dooley, a former salesman and substitute teacher who became Foster's CIS project manager in 2000, encouraged Spearman and five other Foster parents to attend Project GRAD's Parent University training. "That was the best thing that ever happened," Spearman said. "It gave all the parents input about how to make the school and the feeder system better, what programs we needed, what would make the parents more comfortable working with the school."

The six parents wanted to start an after-school program at Foster. They were troubled by the large number of latchkey children they saw in the neighborhood with nothing to do between the time school was dismissed and the time when their parents returned home from work. Through Parent University, the Foster contingent met groups from other Project GRAD schools and discovered that they had similar concerns. Together, they learned how to write grant applications and how to address school and community leaders. The Foster parents eventually received a 2-year grant from the Texas Metropolitan Organization to create an after-school center offering homework assistance and classes in drama, dance, computers, and Spanish.

Many days, Spearman said, about 300 students attended the sessions. "I think it had a lot of impact on academics because we had standards and guidelines," she said. "To come, you had to have an average of C or above and not have any discipline problems or more than three unexcused absences. It gave the kids something to strive for. When those who had behavioral problems passed by and saw kids doing dance, they wanted to be part of it. So they'd come up and say, 'Look at my report card. See how much better I'm doing.'"

From the Parent University, Spearman also got the idea to sponsor a family education night at the school. Parents showed up for a series of short classes, including sessions about the Project GRAD curricular components. Then, after presenting their stamps for good attendance in each class, they earned tickets to a spaghetti supper in the cafeteria with their children.

To Spearman, such activities show formerly powerless parents how they can have a direct impact on their children's education and become a catalyst for school change. When Foster joined Project GRAD in 1996, it had among the lowest student achievement levels in the Yates feeder system, and by 2000 it had dropped to the bottom of the pack as other schools surged ahead. Since then, Foster has made steady progress. The number of students who passed the Texas annual reading test rose from 65% in 2000 to 80% in 2001, and to 93% in 2002. In math, 58% of Foster's students passed the state's annual test in 2000, 79% passed in 2001, and 92% passed in 2002. Foster's performance on the 2002 exams earned the school exemplary status, the highest of four rankings given by the Texas Education Agency.

Foster's faculty played a critical part in the school's transformation, but the spark came from a teacher who simultaneously looked through the lens of a parent. With two children at Foster, physical education teacher Frederick Terrell saw how much more they learned when teachers followed Project GRAD's recommendations. At the same time, he knew that some of his colleagues were resisting the changes. During the 1999–2000 school year, Terrell brought the faculty together for a meeting and told his colleagues that it was time to take Foster to new heights. He agreed to do his part by switching back to teaching math, his specialty, and he subsequently set up a math lab for 3rd through 5th graders to reinforce concepts they were missing on the state tests.

Some of his colleagues "did get upset because they didn't want to make the changes," Terrell said, but the commitment from the majority made it increasingly difficult for others to lag behind. "The first thing I noticed was more parent involvement. That showed me that teachers were getting more in contact with the parents."

One of the newly involved parents was Clinton J. "Lonnie" Long who had grown up in a nearby housing project with Robert Dooley and was among the first black students in the formerly all-white neighborhood to attend college in the early 1970s. In 2001, Long moved back home with his mother after his father died, and subsequently enrolled his son, Levi, at Foster. Long noticed almost immediately that the school had higher expectations than the one his son had attended since kindergarten. His son's former teachers often commented on the boy's intelligence, but they seemed satisfied that he was earning C's and B's.

At Foster, by contrast, Levi's 3rd-grade teacher expected excellence. "When I got to Foster and was introduced to Project GRAD, one of the things they suggested to me right off the top was to be a partner with his classroom teacher," Long said. "That made a big impact. I had never thought of myself as a partner with the teacher. At the old school, I just picked him up and dropped him off each day."

Soon, Long realized just how much collaboration and commitment Foster had in mind. After bringing Levi to school, Long stayed around to observe his teacher, Gloria Lawson, and later asked her questions about his son's progress. When Lawson told him that Levi's chattering was interfering with his studies, Long demanded better behavior from his child. He also heeded Lawson's advice about reinforcing lessons at home, probed his son's homework assignments, made him revise any work that he considered beneath his ability, and helped him study for tests. As a result, Levi turned his C's into A's and earned a perfect score on the state achievement tests given at the end of 3rd grade.

Long's regular presence at Foster also had a positive effect on other children. Robert Dooley recalled the time he stopped at Long's house and found a swarm of young boys engaged in an animated book discussion with Long in the front yard. "This is amazing. In the summer!" said Dooley, who immediately hatched a plan to continue the book discussions during the school year. "That in itself has shown the impact, as he has become accepted" by children who "don't have fathers around."

Although Long and Spearman are the most recognizable parents on Foster's campus, other adults have volunteered to read to students at school, serve as crossing guards, staff an information desk near the office, and form a school safety team called Parents on Patrol. The safety crew members—four grandfathers and a grandmother who were recruited during the school's annual Walk for Success—make sure the children get to class on time and monitor the school grounds.

Parents on Patrol member Tommie McGowan, a retired truck driver whose children and grandchildren attended Foster, often spends 6 to 8 hours a day at the school. He created a chart of each teacher's schedule so he could tell parents exactly where their children are at any time of the day, and he encourages parents to interact with the students, even if they have just a few minutes to walk down the hall and smile. Likewise, McGowan expects the students to contribute a positive attitude and maximum effort each day.

"I want to let the kids know that education is important," he said. "Nothing is free. They have to work for this, show some effort. It doesn't matter who you are, if you step forward, someone will help you."

Dooley said that Foster students practically race to show McGowan and other adult volunteers their report cards to earn praise or a hug. With each interaction, the avuncular adults groom the children for success.

"The idea that a child can't learn is not acceptable" at Foster, Dooley said. "If they can listen to the radio and sing the words of every hip-hop song out there, they can learn MOVE IT Math and Success for All. I state that and I believe that. Being from a high-poverty background is not an excuse."

FROM ONE TO MANY

Similar success stories are easy to find in buildings served by Communities in Schools, and become one of the biggest selling points for districts that are exploring partnerships with Project GRAD. Educators generally recognize that no matter how strong a school's instructional components might be, students won't learn much if their parents are in crisis or uninvolved.

At the same time, CIS is one of the most expensive programmatic components of Project GRAD, representing about 23% of the $500-per-student cost because of the additional full-time staff members required for each center. (According to Project GRAD, a typical feeder system of 10,000 students will incur costs of $5.3 million—$532 per child per year—during the 4-year curriculum installation phase. After 5 years of participation, the cost of the program is about $320 per child.) This is not to say that Communities in Schools' costs are excessive; only that educators may perceive them to be high compared to other reform expenses. By most accounts, CIS does an admirable job of providing services to students and their families. In 2002 and 2003, *Worth* magazine named Communities in Schools one of the nation's 100 best charities, noting that for every $100 donated to the organization, $90 goes directly to programs. But CIS also has an indirect impact on student achievement, so its costs are harder to justify in schools desperately trying to raise test scores.

CIS doesn't operate in every school affiliated with Project GRAD. Project GRAD–Los Angeles calls its school support centers "Connections" because leaders thought the existing Communities in Schools organization in Los Angeles focused too much on dropout-prevention strategies and not enough on academic enrichment. Other Project GRAD cities, including Cincinnati, Knoxville, and Akron, call their social services component "Campus Family Support." Project GRAD developed the Campus Family Support program for cities that did not already have Communities in Schools organizations.

Establishing uniform practices in all the social services support centers has proved challenging for Project GRAD. Cities that joined after Project GRAD–USA formed in 2001 signed contracts that spelled out the expectations for the social services component. Each center is supposed to provide crisis intervention, tutoring, and mentoring for students, develop parent involvement activities, and form community partnerships. Secondary school centers are also supposed to stress college awareness and preparation.

Those goals weren't clearly defined when Project GRAD started, however. And in some cases, tensions surfaced over whose vision the campus support teams should fulfill—Project GRAD's, the school principal's, or the local organization's.

In Los Angeles, Project GRAD executive director Cheryl Mabey (who died in March 2004) reorganized the Connections program in 2002 after growing frustrated at the limited impact it was having. Up to that point, Connections staff members had used a case-management approach that required them to complete about 17 pages of legal documentation per child to justify the services they were providing. Keeping up with the voluminous paperwork meant they could serve only about 30 students in the smaller schools and about 90 students in the larger ones.

"That's not enough," said Mabey, who pointed out that some case managers were using the process as a sorting mechanism to weed out children who needed assistance that their programs didn't routinely cover. She continued, "Middle schools have the worst problem. They're afraid they'll have hundreds of kids dumped on them."

Mabey took the Connections staff members to a weekend retreat in November 2002 where they focused on developing school-wide interventions, such as the Walk for Success and after-school math labs available to all 9th graders, not just those who are part of the case management files. "If they're a Project GRAD employee, they must focus on the entire school," Mabey said.

Social services managers acknowledge the difficulty of providing quality assistance to large numbers of students, and they constantly fret about whether they're making the intimate connections that research suggests keeps children out of trouble.

At Malcolm X. Shabazz High School in Newark, New Jersey, Communities in Schools operated a center on campus for 4 years before Shabazz became the first local feeder system to join Project GRAD. Because Project GRAD emphasizes school-wide interventions, the CIS staff had to switch from working consistently with about 150 students to working occasionally with the entire population.

Natasha Wright Eldridge, the CIS project director at Shabazz, said, "Kids who were part of the one hundred and fifty didn't want to be told that twelve hundred other kids needed you, too." Eldridge tried to integrate the two approaches by setting up a series of programs that would reach large numbers of students throughout the school year but focus on small groups at any one time. For example, she and her associate director use their vacation time and recruit parent volunteers to take 20 to 30 low-performing juniors and seniors on college visits. These students don't qualify for Project GRAD scholarships because of their low grade-point averages, so they might otherwise fall through the cracks. CIS helps them complete college applications and financial aid forms, then writes letters of recommendation and lobbies on their behalf with admissions officers. After the students enroll in college, CIS stays in touch with them, sending them care packages of detergent and food and monitoring their academic progress. CIS also posts the students' college-acceptance letters in the office to demonstrate to subsequent classes what their perseverance can produce.

Recognizing that many Shabazz students couldn't read or write well but were too embarrassed to ask for help, the CIS staff recruited an English teacher to start a tutoring program whose meeting time and location are known only to the participants. The program proved so successful that Eldridge added math and Spanish language tutoring sessions during the 2002–03 school year and hired two part-time reading tutors to handle the increasing number of students seeking assistance.

A principal's relationship with CIS staff members is extremely important to the success of the social services program, but in some schools administrators have been openly hostile to the social workers and counselors. CIS directors encourage the school-based project managers to build close ties by meeting at least once a month with the principal, although the most successful partnerships involve more frequent contact. To improve the consistency of services within the feeder systems, CIS also holds monthly meetings of all project managers and counselors and follows up with students when they leave for the next grade level.

Yet CIS can't control all the problems that affect students' success. For example, CIS has no authority to challenge administrators and staff when their abrasive behavior makes students afraid to ask for help, to remove teachers who continually scream at children in and out of class, or to stop the high turnover of teachers that leads to inconsistent instruction.

Part of the challenge—and part of the strength—of CIS is that its staff works *with* school officials yet operates *independently* from them. Acting as a broker between the school and the family, CIS can be seen as a healer or an antagonist, depending on the observer's perspective about family involvement in education.

As researchers noted in the recent national report *Strong Neighborhoods Strong Schools*, low-income families have had limited experience and assistance playing a meaningful role in their children's schools, primarily because those institutions tend to be insular places cut off from new ideas and public accountability (Gold, Simon, & Brown, 2002).

"Bureaucracies, such as city government and urban school systems, are known for inaction, corruption, and resistance to change," the report noted. "The structure of accountability can be diffuse, making it possible for officials to pass responsibility off, one to another. In addition, school and public officials manage competing interests, and they often act in their own best interest—avoiding the risk of losing power."

University of Chicago professors Anthony S. Byrk and Barbara Schneider go further, arguing that schools cannot sustain improvements until and unless members of the school community develop strong relationships based on mutual respect and trust. Using data to demonstrate the links between trust levels and academic achievement, Byrk and Schneider argue that strong connections enable schools to mobilize resources for children (Gewertz, 2002).

To be most effective, parents and their advocates need to work in concert with educators in planning and coordinating services for children. To nurture these partnerships, noted Javier Parra, Project GRAD–Houston's manager for parent and community involvement for secondary schools, the staff of CIS must spend time understanding the dynamics, including the unspoken problems, of each school community. "In every school we have to look at the culture and what moves people," Parra said. "Two schools can be only seven blocks apart but have completely different cultures."

If parents feel unwelcome in a school, for example, CIS might need to hold get-acquainted meetings in a neutral setting, such as a community center, until trust builds. Or organizers might sponsor an uplifting event, such as a student recognition ceremony, so parents will see that the school building is more than the site of frequent showdowns. Another option would be to involve a respected community leader who can bring the disputing parties to peace.

Parra noted, "One thing we have forgotten about [in this country] is that there are very few institutions that represent the community and hold it together. . . . The first is the family, the second is the church, and sometimes these don't exist for kids, so they'll make up their own institution and join gangs. The school can be that community institution. It's like an extended capacity of learning for the kids."

Some schools "forget" to do community building, Parra said. They don't seek partnerships with civic groups and parents and don't work well when community members offer assistance: "The more we have people working at education, the better job we'll all do. It's an investment for all of us. If someone says we don't need that, they're wrong."

WALK FOR SUCCESS

On March, 22, 2002, leaders of Project GRAD announced that Sam Houston High School would become the latest and largest feeder system in Houston, adding 16,000 students to the list of those eligible for scholarships. For the public announcement, which was held in an auditorium on the University of Houston's main campus, Project GRAD brought in busloads of students, parents, and educators from across the Sam Houston feeder system. During the assembly, Sam Houston High School principal Roberto Gonzalez explained in both English and Spanish the standard he expects students to meet. A former assistant principal at Davis High School and a former principal at Marshall Middle School, Gonzalez said he witnessed the transformation of schools in the Davis feeder system and lobbied to get Sam Houston into Project GRAD.

"Last year, so you understand the importance of Project GRAD to a system like ours, Sam Houston High School graduates received forty-seven [college] scholarships that totaled about $500,000," Gonzalez told the audience. "By comparison, in another school, just down the road from us, Jeff Davis High School, that has half the number of students that we have, they were offered and received one hundred ninety scholarships that totaled more than two million dollars. That is the importance of this program to you."

Later, after the assembly had ended, Gonzalez circulated among the students who were milling in the aisles. He reminded the teenagers that volunteers would be walking in their neighborhoods the following morning to explain the Project GRAD scholarship program. Be ready, he told them. Tell your parents that the volunteers are coming. Make sure you're home when they stop by.

Some of the students responded positively. A few shook the principal's hand. But to one group of insouciant teenagers, Gonzalez might have been talking to a brick wall.

"We ain't got no windows," one girl said belligerently.

"We ain't got no door," another girl added, emboldened by her peer. "You can't knock on it."

Gonzalez, looking completely unflappable, didn't even pause to think. "Well, then," he said with a smile and a nod to the girls, " I'll just knock on the doorframe instead."

At 8 a.m. the next morning, the parking lot at Sam Houston High School was so crowded with cars that some people drove their vehicles onto the grassy medians and concrete curbs surrounding the school. Observers looked on in amazement, wondering what could have motivated so many people to get out of bed this early on a Saturday morning.

The common cause was the Walk for Success, an annual event among Project GRAD schools and the first for the Sam Houston feeder system. During the Walk for Success, volunteers fan out in the neighborhoods surrounding the school, knocking on doors to meet with families, discussing the benefits and requirements of the college scholarship offer and asking parents and students to sign a pledge of participation.

Such face-to-face contact is an important part of the effort to break down the traditional barriers that discourage many urban parents from getting involved in their children's education. When school representatives meet families on their own turf, they symbolically shed the mantel of authority that can intimidate parents who have limited education and memories of failure in school. By ensuring that each volunteer group includes at least one Spanish-speaking member and carries documents in both English and Spanish, Project GRAD also demonstrates respect for language differences instead of expecting families to make all the accommodations. In addition, the volunteers distribute surveys to find out if families need assistance. Project GRAD uses the information to design workshops, arrange classes, and make referrals to other agencies.

Although the Walk for Success is only one of many programs that Communities in Schools (CIS) coordinates for Project GRAD, it has proven so effective at building bridges that CIS uses it in many Houston schools that are not part of Project GRAD. "You're getting the message out that schools care about you," explained Cynthia Clay Briggs, executive director of Communities in Schools Houston. "When you go to someone instead of waiting for them to come to you, it's very empowering."

Preparing the Walk for Success is a time-consuming process that involves recruiting and training hundreds of volunteers, culling through lists of students' addresses, arranging the names in clusters that people can contact within a few hours, and preparing packets of materials, including suggested scripts. In the weeks leading up to a Walk for Success, CIS representatives discuss the upcoming visits with students. They also send notices to families by mail, and follow up by telephone. Occasionally, they will stand at the curb when parents drop off their children at school and speak to them through car windows. On the day of the walk, the organizers bring breakfast and lunch for the volunteers, arrange free entertainment from school and community groups, then hope for good weather and a strong turnout. For a multischool Walk for Success in October 2001, 2,700 Houston volunteers visited 7,600 homes on a single Saturday morning.

The Walk for Success also builds a constituency for Project GRAD. When organizers recruit professors and college students to assist with the walk, they gain allies who can help smooth the high school-college transition for students. When they recruit people from local businesses and government, they tap into sources for mentoring and donations. When they recruit parents and other neighborhood residents, they find a base of support for improvements that can affect the entire community.

"Deep community-school relationships combine *inside* expertise with *outside* resources and support," concluded a study of urban school partnerships conducted for the Rockefeller Foundation (Jehl, Blank, & McCloud, 2001). "They have a dual benefit: By expanding the services, supports, and opportunities available to young people, they increase their opportunities for learning and development; by strengthening the school as the universally available public institution in the community, they increase assets to community residents."

Because so many volunteers showed up for the inaugural Walk for Success at Sam Houston High, each group was responsible for contacting only five or six families. Sergio Montelongo, who was then Project GRAD's financial aid coordinator at Davis High School, led a group that included Herrera Elementary School principal Hector Rodriguez and Victor Flores and Huý Vu, a sophomore and senior, respectively, at Reagan High School. Montelongo and Rodriguez both speak Spanish and had participated in several previous walks. Huý, participating in his second event, showed up to earn some community service hours. And Victor said he wanted to give back to a program that had promised to send him to college.

As Montelongo consulted the list of homes that the group was supposed to visit, Rodriguez drove the four volunteers in his van. At the first house, a locked fence surrounded the property and two dogs barked menacingly as the Project GRAD group approached. Using his cell phone, Montelongo called the number listed for the family. A few minutes later, a middle-aged woman opened the gate for the visitors and led them inside the house.

The woman said she has six children. One of the girls was in college and another had dropped out to care for her newborn. The mother listened intently as Montelongo and Rodriguez spoke to her in Spanish about Project GRAD. Then she went to a back room to retrieve her son, the 9th grader whose future the visitors hoped to ensure with a college scholarship.

"It's a good deal, amigo," Rodriguez said to the sleepy teenager, switching to English. "This is going to help you get to college." When the teenager said he wanted to be a police officer, Rodriguez told him that a university degree would make him a more valuable employee, whatever career he pursued.

Montelongo described the summer institute that the boy would attend through Project GRAD, adding that students' grades usually improved when they returned to their high schools in the fall. Then he described the $150 stipend each student receives at the conclusion of the summer program.

With assistance from her daughter, the mother proceeded to fill out the survey that Montelongo handed to her. She expressed an interest in attending classes that would show her how to help her children with their homework, and she asked if the high school could employ bilingual staff members who could translate when Spanish-speaking parents were in the building.

Rodriguez praised the woman for encouraging her older children to go to college and for staying in touch with all of her children's schools. The mother thanked the men for giving her son the opportunity to earn a scholarship, then proceeded to shake each of the visitors' hands.

When no one answered the knock at the next house on the list, the group moved on to the third home, which was also surrounded by a locked fence. Montelongo brought out his cell phone again and called the family.

"Oh, the scholarship," the mother said in Spanish, motioning to a child standing by. "Don't just stand there. Open the door."

After unlocking the gate, the family stood in the driveway to talk, explaining that the house was too messy to invite everyone inside. The mother said she had emigrated from Mexico but that her children were born in Texas. The oldest of her three children stood sullenly off to the side. Asked by Rodriguez how he liked Sam Houston High School, the 9th grader shrugged.

"It's better than nothing," he said.

Because his grades were low, the boy said he hadn't considered going to college. "I'm not even worried about that right now. I'm just worried about this year, getting through algebra."

On the survey, the boy's mother indicated that she would attend English, math, and computer classes for adults and wanted guidance about disciplining her children. She told the visitors that the only time she visited their schools was when one of the children got in trouble.

As the conversation ended, she smiled and thanked the visitors for coming to her home. She told them that no one had ever talked to her before about college.

At the next address, a dilapidated trailer perched on a weed-covered lot, Montelongo's knocks brought no reply. The last house on the list produced an older Latino father who said he doubted that his rebellious 9th grader would live up to Project GRAD's requirements. He explained that his 20-year-old daughter had reluctantly obtained her high school equivalency certificate but had no ambition, and his younger daughter seemed determined to follow her sister's example.

Rodriguez engaged the man in a lengthy conversation about the benefits that would come to the Sam Houston feeder system because of Project GRAD, including curriculum changes and school social workers.

"You can have all the kinds of programs you want," the father said stubbornly, "but the motivation has to come from the child."

"You are right on all accounts, sir," Rodriguez said soothingly, patting the frustrated father on the back. "We all control our own destinies. But when children are young, they need help from us."

Several more minutes of dialogue brought them no closer to a resolution, so Rodriguez politely thanked the man for his time and urged him to check out the college scholarship for his daughter.

By the time the four walkers returned to Sam Houston High School shortly after noon, the informal conversations they had initiated between stops had grown into an easy camaraderie. Huý learned from Montelongo, a recent University of Texas graduate, about the best dormitories to seek when he enrolled there in the fall. Rodriguez, who listened to Montelongo's descriptions of effective parent education classes offered through Project GRAD, asked for the younger man's help in starting some sessions at Herrera Elementary School. And after hearing Montelongo tell parents that Texas students who graduate in the top 10% of their high school classes are eligible for state-funded college scholarships, Victor vowed to work harder in school so he could improve his class ranking.

Before signing the Project GRAD pledge the previous summer, Victor said, "I was hanging out with my friends and not studying much. Now I have higher grades and am on the honor roll. I try harder. Instead of talking to my friends in class, I start to pay more attention. I want a better life."

Chapter 5

CLASSROOM CONSISTENCY

In the early 1990s, Marshall Middle School was such a poor place for learning that students routinely threw desks and chairs out the window, bashed in classroom walls, and slipped out of the school building in the middle of the day. Several times a week, administrators would drive the streets surrounding Marshall, searching for truants. When they returned the students to school to be punished, the administrators received not thanks from the faculty but complaints that they had let the miscreants back in the building.[1]

Students often cursed at their teachers, and some educators shouted obscenities in return. The youngsters sprayed their anger and frustration all over the building, defacing school property with graffiti that covered the walls, the lockers, the ceilings, the floors, and the insides of toilet bowls. When the bell signaled the start of each class period, so many Marshall students stayed in the hallways to fight, participate in gang rituals, and otherwise avoid instruction that it seemed the majority spent more time out of their desks than in them. Achievement levels were among the lowest in the Houston school district, with only 20% of Marshall's students meeting all of the state's academic standards in 1994, compared with a 55% state average and a 36% district average for the middle grades (*Academic Excellence Indicator System 1994 Campus Report*, 1995).

Staff morale was nearly nonexistent. Marshall had earned a reputation as a repository for ineffective teachers. Some instructors would leave their classrooms unattended during the school day to go shopping. Staff members often carried arguments into the school parking lot and occasionally came to blows.

"Anything that could have gone wrong did," said Dr. Kimberly Agnew, who started teaching reading at the school in 1993 and later became an assistant principal. "People weren't even trying to get along. There were arguments in the faculty lounge, veteran teachers not helping new teachers. Teachers being very lethargic, not going into the halls [between classes] . . . a lot of gossiping and negative conversation about the administration."

A new principal arrived in 1992 and, with the superintendent's backing, transferred some staff members to other schools. He also made building repairs, initiated regular professional development, and began calling the police for backup whenever students got out of control. With sirens blaring, officers arrived several times a day to issue tickets and haul disruptive students away in handcuffs.

"We wanted that," said Dr. Billie Kennedy, the former dean of instruction who had resorted to subduing students by putting them in headlocks or hurling them against the wall.

Although the previous principal had initiated some important changes, including writing a handbook of school policies and procedures and placing teachers and students on teams to foster camaraderie and interdisciplinary instruction, Marshall remained "extremely dysfunctional," Kennedy said. "And no matter how hard we worked, we couldn't get a handle on it at all."

During the 1993–94 school year, Marshall's administrators began discussions with Jim Ketelsen and Emily Cole about adopting the changes they had initiated at Davis High School. The first component of the new Project GRAD model that Marshall's staff agreed to try was Consistency Management & Cooperative Discipline® (CMCD®) because getting students to behave was first among a long list of priorities at the school.

Restoring order often is the first response when troubled schools attempt turnarounds, which is why Project GRAD included a classroom management program among its major components. Despite external pressure to raise test scores, many schools that join Project GRAD want to adopt Consistency Management first because they understand that their current chaos stifles learning. Nationally, 25% of 8th-grade teachers in urban schools report spending one fifth of their instructional time on discipline, which is twice the rate for teachers in rural schools and one third more than for suburban teachers (Lippman et al., 1996). From the students' perspective, only 38% of urban students nationally describe their schools as safe, while 42% say their classrooms are so noisy they have a difficult time concentrating (MetLife, Inc., 2001). Among those students who rate the quality of teaching in their schools as low, the perceived school safety level falls to 26%.

Along with unclear rules, irregular enforcement of punishments, and limited cooperation among teachers and administrators, the common reasons for school discipline problems are large, impersonal schools that offer few resources to teachers and show little concern for students as individuals (Gaustad, 1992). Researchers have found that school discipline has a strong bearing on student achievement. Higher levels of both major (such as weapons possession) and minor (such as tardiness) offenses in a school correlate with lower gains in student achievement (Mayer, Mullens, & Moore, 2000).

Yet harsh discipline policies are not consistent deterrents to misbehavior, as Marshall's experience shows. The strongest motivation for students to learn and stay out of trouble is engaging and challenging instruction from teachers who care about them.

University of Houston education professor H. Jerome Freiberg developed Consistency Management after years of researching strategies that enable teachers and students to excel. Many of the methods he created or adapted aren't unique; effective teachers typically use similar techniques to build relationships with students and keep them interested in their work. Freiberg's major contribution was developing a system of effective strategies that many teachers, particularly those in urban schools, haven't learned or practiced. Then he connected the system to a philosophy of education that places students at the center of teachers' decisions.

"Consistency Management, I think it's the best thing on the market for classroom management," said Dr. Donald R. McAdams, author of *Fighting to Save Our Urban Schools . . . and Winning!* (Teachers College Press, 2000) and former president of the Board of Education for the Houston Independent School District. He continued, "When you take the common sense and systemize it and thoroughly train people, you get results. What is surprising is that [many] teachers don't do that on their own."

The American Federation of Teachers (1998b) named Consistency Management one of six promising school-wide reform programs and one of five promising discipline and violence prevention programs in the country (American Federation of Teachers, 2000). Groups such as the U.S.

Department of Education, the Center for Evaluation at Harvard University, Johns Hopkins University's Center for Research on the Education of Students Placed at Risk, and the Center for the Study of Violence Prevention at the University of Colorado have evaluated CMCD and cited its impact on improving student discipline and achievement. Additional research has shown a strong link between CMCD's ability to increase students' feelings of belonging in school and their improved behavior (McNeely, Nonnemaker, & Blum, 2002).

At its core, Consistency Management is about respecting the right of every child to play an active role in the classroom. Traditionally, Freiberg says, teachers have relied on about 20% of the students in their classes to participate in class discussions, act as helpers and monitors, and assume various leadership positions. The remaining 80% usually have no investment in the class and either tune out the lecture or learn that causing trouble is the only way to get attention.

Consistency Management seeks to change those patterns so students move from passive recipients of knowledge (which Freiberg calls "tourists") to active participants in the organization and management of their learning (which Freiberg calls "citizens"). Instead of trying to control students by establishing prohibitions, Consistency Management shows teachers and other adults in the school how to involve them in creating a classroom culture that encourages and recognizes good behavior. Teachers and students jointly determine rights and responsibilities and work to support them.

For example, every 6 to 8 weeks students in CMCD classrooms formally apply for a series of mutually determined "consistency manager" positions that can range from classroom greeter and homework collector to technology specialist and sharpener of pencils. By delegating these jobs to students, teachers can concentrate on instruction instead of discipline. When the setup becomes routine, students perform their jobs and start their assignments as soon as they enter the classroom instead of wasting time trying to figure out the sequence of the day's events.

Students "don't learn self-discipline if they're always dependent on someone telling them what to do," Freiberg says. "Kids need to learn to function the same whether they are with adults or not."

After some initial training by Freiberg in the fall of 1994, the Marshall faculty voted by secret ballot to adopt the program (Agnew, 2001). Ninety-two percent of the teachers voted yes. CMCD requires at least 70% of the staff to choose to participate before starting.

Teachers approved CMCD "not necessarily because they favored the program and its components, but because they were desperate for a change," Agnew wrote in her doctoral dissertation about the process. "Survival was the ongoing theme, and everybody was ready to be rescued."

Before the faculty voted to adopt CMCD, Freiberg met with the Marshall teachers to discuss his philosophy of discipline and instruction and to suggest practical methods they could use. He also collected baseline data about the school's climate, including statistics on suspensions and office referrals and survey information from students, teachers, and administrators.

Prior to implementing CMCD, Shell Oil paid the tuition and book fees for about 25 teachers to take a graduate-level course with Freiberg based on his book *Universal Teaching Strategies*. Freiberg then provided Consistency Management training to Marshall's full faculty in the spring of 1995 to prepare them for using the program the following term. Once they did so, Kennedy said, "The difference was night and day."

One of those who benefited from the switch was Craig Landwehr, a reading teacher who had endured a "baptism by fire" during his tumultuous first year at Marshall in 1993. He remembers observing at least one fight a day in the hallways—"very physical altercations, blood, bruises"— and similar chaos in his classroom, where students threw dictionaries and papers out the window when his back was turned. Although school leaders assigned Landwehr a teacher-mentor who "gave me a lot of help and ideas," collectively the staff didn't have the time or the skills to show him how to manage his classes effectively. "It was such a rough year," he said. The students "had smelled fresh meat and were ready for the kill."

The following summer, Landwehr enrolled in graduate education courses at the University of Houston and began searching for ways to improve his teaching. When he started the 1994–95 school year at Marshall, he was better prepared, demonstrating a firmer hand with students from the first day. Yet he said that initially he was "so heady with the thought that I could have a class be quiet" that he didn't realize making students read silently for long stretches wasn't going to keep them interested or compliant.

As he studied CMCD and consulted with Freiberg, Landwehr said he learned that his initial attempts at classroom management had emphasized control more than involvement. He had learned to be consistent with his instructions and policies, so students were no longer confused about what they were supposed to do each day. But he wasn't using cooperative groups to teach them how to function in a democracy. He hadn't given students choices so they could explore topics and express their understanding through a range of sources and evaluations. And he didn't trust them enough to let everyone have a say in how the class was run.

Like many inexperienced teachers, Landwehr initially had assumed that he must always be in charge. He lacked the self-confidence to let his students' interests and questions help shape their education. Unconsciously or not, he had judged them incapable of making good decisions without the authoritarian influence of the teacher.

When the 1995–96 school year started, Landwehr embedded Consistency Management's practices into his instruction. He showed his students the program's classroom Magna Carta, which spells out the fundamental rights of all students to be treated fairly, to express their opinions, and to be safe in the classroom. Then, together, Landwehr and his students created a constitution that specified the rules and roles necessary to fulfill the Magna Carta pledge. The guidelines they selected weren't distinctive from many classrooms, Landwehr recalled, because by the time they reach middle school adolescents have become "professional students" who know they're supposed to raise their hands before speaking, ask permission to leave the classroom, and refrain from cheating on tests. The difference this time was that they got to help choose the terms.

As students practiced the classroom routines, Landwehr provided feedback about their progress, "not gushy or unrealistic" comments but genuine praise for their initiative, their follow-through, and their commitment to learning. Over and over, he told them that "'learning is the most important thing that happens in this room, whether I'm here, or a substitute [teacher] is here, or no one is here.'"

Although he felt good about the changes, it took his absence from school one day to appreciate the deeper transformation that was occurring. When one of his own children became ill about 8 weeks into the new term and needed a physician's attention, Landwehr called the school district's substitute teacher hotline and asked for a temporary replacement. He assumed the request would be honored. Instead, students in Landwehr's 7th-grade reading class found no one in charge when they arrived for the first period. Undeterred, the children calmly performed their classroom management jobs, filed into their seats, and began working on the assignment that Landwehr had posted the day before. When another teacher passed by and saw that Landwehr was absent, he told the students to continue working and to contact him if they needed anything.

Near the end of the 90-minute period, Billie Kennedy discovered that the substitute teacher had not arrived and so she raced upstairs to Landwehr's classroom.

"I was really worried," she said. But instead of finding a class in chaos, she opened the door and saw students quietly writing at their desks. She recalled that they said, "Dr. Kennedy, everything is okay. You can leave us alone."

The substitute teacher showed up a short time later, and the day proceeded so smoothly that no one thought to inform Landwehr of his students' good behavior when he returned to Marshall the following morning. Two days later, however, when he was reading the students' journal reflections that they wrote at the end of every class, he gained new insights about their growing self-reliance. "I feel sad because Mr. Landwehr is absent today," one student wrote in his journal entry. "The good thing is that nobody is behaving bad. Everybody was doing the work." Another student said she was happy "because no one's here and the room is so quiet. We're all doing what we're suppose [sic] to." "I feel lucky today because the day has just started and we have already been trusted in something we have never been trusted on, being alone," a third student wrote. "It is 8:15 and every thing is cool. Nothing is even wrong. There is silense [sic] in the room."

To Landwehr, the incident was all the more remarkable because the class included some of the lowest-performing students in the school, the same kind of adolescents who traditionally caused most of the disruptions. Only 18% of his students had passed a diagnostic reading test that he had given them at the beginning of the school year. Nine months later, he said, 68% of his students met the state's grade-level standard in reading.

Such progress aside, misbehavior and low achievement didn't automatically disappear at Marshall in 1995. Fights still broke out from time to time, and some teachers remained skeptical that the students were capable of excelling. But success eventually wore down resistance. Landwehr and other teachers shared their students' accomplishments at CMCD work-shops and staff meetings, trying to inspire by example.

Marshall's daily team planning sessions helped. Landwehr recalled one meeting when teachers were commiserating about Daniel, a highly so-ciable student who roamed the halls and always arrived late to class. Then one teacher reported that she had made Daniel the Consistency Manage-ment tardy manager, responsible for checking whether students came to class on time. Because he had an important job to perform, which included listing his own attention to the clock, Daniel hadn't been late to class since, the teacher said.

As staff members sought similar solutions and stopped blaming the stu-dents for Marshall's poor performance, achievement and attitudes improved throughout the school. When Kwame Opuni, the University of St. Thomas researcher, measured the changes in the school's climate from 1996 to 1998, he found that eight of ten indicators on the Comprehensive Assessment of School Environment had risen from well below the national average to within or beyond the normal range (Opuni & Ochoa, 2002a). The highest scores occurred in the category of teacher-student relations. Security and maintenance remained the only concerns. Moreover, Marshall's teachers reported that they saved an average of 30 minutes per day for instruction—an extra 15 days a year—because they no longer had to waste time resolv-ing disciplinary problems (Opuni, 2001). From 1996 to 1999, the number of discipline referrals at Marshall was cut in half (Agnew, 2001).

To solve some of the remaining problems, Marshall's staff invited the most disinterested and uninvolved youngsters from each grade level to form school-improvement clubs, which Consistency Management calls "Student Cadres." Members of one Student Cadre decided to become goodwill am-bassadors for the school, opening doors for teachers in the morning and conducting tours for elementary students. One Student Cadre performed commercials for the school's morning television show, and another decided to make greeting cards for teachers to celebrate birthdays and holidays. When Marshall adopted school uniforms, a Student Cadre offered to spon-sor a fashion show to demonstrate the various clothing options.

The attention to good behavior soon extended beyond the school build-ing. Carmen Nuncio, a parent who reluctantly sent her youngest child to Marshall after steering her three oldest daughters to other schools, recalled the day she received a postcard telling her how her daughter had performed as the class attendance manager. "You are home getting your mail, getting your bills, and you get something like that, it just makes you feel so proud," Nuncio said in an interview with the *Houston Chronicle*. She later became a regular volunteer at the school she had previously shunned (Markley, 1996).

Former and current staff members believe CMCD acted as a catalyst for significant cultural changes at Marshall that continue to this day. CMCD was the first component of Project GRAD at Marshall, and it laid the foundation for the rest of the reform framework. From 1994 to 2002, the percentage of Marshall's students meeting the state's grade-level standards in all the tested subjects more than tripled and surpassed both district and state averages (*Academic Excellence Indicator System*, 1995). On national standardized tests, Marshall's students improved in both math and reading, but not to the degree indicated on the state's exams (Opuni & Ochoa, 2002b). Nevertheless, all the academic signs pointed upward.

A FRAMEWORK FOR GOOD BEHAVIOR

Like many teachers, Jerome Freiberg learned how to manage a classroom over time, mostly through trial and error in some of the roughest schools in the Northeast. Early in his career, he taught high school in Philadelphia and Chester, Pennsylvania and worked as a substitute teacher at a combined junior-senior high school in rural Massachusetts. In 1971, while completing a doctoral degree in education, he taught world history at a middle school in Providence, Rhode Island and at night volunteered to teach inmates at a maximum-security prison in Warwick.

At the middle school, administrators chose Freiberg to be the leader of a team of new teachers. Only later did he discover that some veteran educators had created the team's class lists, giving Freiberg and the other newcomers some of the worst troublemakers in the building. During an early field trip to a local fine arts museum, Freiberg's students caused such a disturbance when they came upon some nude statues that the museum guards "asked us to leave and the bus driver wouldn't take us home."

Freiberg was so angry that he told his students he would never take them on another field trip. But after reflecting, he realized that part of the fault was his: He hadn't prepared the students well for the outing. He discovered that the students had never been to an art museum before and were both overwhelmed by the displays and unfamiliar with the expected decorum. Like typical adolescents, he said, they hid their awkwardness and their embarrassment by misbehaving. The disturbance they caused stemmed from their confusion about how they were supposed to act. They lacked some of the social skills that children from more privileged backgrounds usually learn through family and cultural connections.

Freiberg began changing his classroom procedures so they would be clearer and more consistent. He involved students in creating a classroom Bill of Rights, color-coded materials for different groups so they would know where to place and retrieve their papers, and made sure to list an assignment on the chalkboard at the start of each period. In the latter case, the short activities he built into the daily sequence related to the larger lessons and were designed to provide quick mental stimulation. Students learned to work on these assignments as soon as they entered the classroom instead of waiting for directions or getting distracted during class changes. Freiberg referred to each of these prompts as "a focus," but other educators call them sponges or warm-up exercises. The name isn't as important as the intent, to maximize the time for instruction instead of letting students wander without a purpose, either intellectually or physically.

One morning, students in Freiberg's 6th-grade history class arrived to find some hieroglyphics on the chalkboard and were instantly curious. He explained that the symbols were from an ancient language they would be studying as part of a unit about Egypt. As they learned how to decipher the code, the students became so engrossed in hieroglyphics that they sometimes used the symbols on notes that they passed in other classes, to the surprise of Freiberg's colleagues.

Toward the end of the Egyptian unit, a student asked Freiberg if he would take the class to see a related exhibit at a Boston art museum. "He said he would never take us on a field trip again," one student blurted out in response, and his classmates nodded in resignation.

That was true, Freiberg reminded them, but then he issued a challenge. "If you want to go to this museum," he said, "you're going to have to take *me*."

At first, the students were stymied because they had never planned such an extensive outing. But Freiberg helped them to break down the process into a series of responsibilities. Every student had a job, whether obtaining permission slips, finding a benefactor to pay for the museum admission fees, or locating road maps to plan the best route. Meanwhile, Freiberg visited the museum alone, took photographic slides of everything the students would see at the exhibit, and brought the slides back to the class to share.

"I did this because it would be a reinforcement," he said later, "and if there were any issues, we could talk about them beforehand."

As part of this prevention strategy, Freiberg brought a large piece of linen cloth to class and passed it around so all the students could touch it. Afterward, he held up the cloth so they would see the smudges left by their fingerprints. He explained that the oils on each person's hands transfer to the cloth and leave stains that accumulate.

"If enough people do that, all these antiquities would be gone. They'd fall apart," Freiberg told his students, explaining why museums ask visitors to refrain from touching exhibits. One student, looking puzzled, told Freiberg: "I thought they didn't want us to touch them because they knew we were bad."

Freiberg said the incident proved as instructive to him as it was to the students: "There were several things I learned from this process. One was that we as teachers don't always find out why kids think the way they think. We don't then respond in a way that's very productive. They needed to know why things happened. They needed an explanation. They just didn't have a context for things because kids don't travel out of their neighborhoods much, particularly if they're impoverished."

Because he took steps to prepare students for the second field trip and involved them in planning it, the outing was a huge success. At one point during the museum tour, the students came upon a large stone tomb that encased a mummy. A red velvet rope, designed to keep observers several feet away, surrounded the exhibit. When the students crowded around the tomb, a security guard shooed them away. One student was transfixed by the tomb, however, and began reading aloud some of the hieroglyphics carved there. Curious, the security guard came closer and asked the boy if he knew what the other symbols represented. The boy's classmates added their interpretations. Instead of furthering their estrangement, the students ended up making friends with the guard by conducting a short history lesson on a topic in which they had considerable expertise.

That school year, in addition to recognizing the necessity of providing clear instructions, consistent guidance, and opportunities for students to demonstrate their skills in realistic settings, Freiberg said he understood the importance that youngsters place on relationships. "Kids didn't want to know what you knew, they wanted to know how much you cared," he said. "If the students don't feel that you're interested in them as people, as individuals, then there's no reason for them to feel interested in you or your subject." He continued, "Those students who have tremendous support at home can maybe get over the barrier of a teacher who doesn't care much about them. But if a kid doesn't have anyone at home and then comes to school and doesn't have anyone who cares about him, then you're really putting that individual at risk."

After the pivotal year teaching middle school in Providence, Freiberg completed his doctorate and began compiling and writing about the techniques he found conducive to a positive classroom climate. The Consistency Management program he created builds from five major themes:

- *Prevention* means that the teacher specifies important classroom procedures and routinely practices them with students, enlisting them as partners in learning.
- *Caring* refers to the practice of surveying students' interests and designing lessons that answer their questions, giving every student opportunities to contribute.
- *Cooperation* means that children and adults assist each other, including working with partners and groups and sharing the responsibility for managing the classroom.
- *Organization* means that the teacher establishes a consistent order of events and activities in the classroom, such as using seating charts, posting homework calendars, and tying all lessons and tests to clearly stated goals.

- *Community* refers to the methods of building the class and team identity, sharing news with students' families, and forming partnerships with local businesses. (Freiberg, 2002)

"This isn't rocket science," Freiberg said, "but it's counterintuitive to what most people do." If what happens in a classroom "only benefits the teachers, the students won't do it. If it only benefits students, teachers burn out. There has to be mutuality."

Consider the role of the classroom managers.[2] In many schools, teachers struggle to prepare lessons, track down resources, and copy materials that need to be distributed each day. When class starts, the teacher herds students into the room, closes the door, and tries to begin the lesson. But two students need to sharpen their pencils and two others forget to bring paper. One student was absent the day before and doesn't know what yesterday's lesson covered or what the teacher assigned for homework. On the intercom, the office staff interrupts and asks the teacher to send down the class attendance list. Handling each of these incidents steals time from the teacher and throws students off task.

Many of these disruptions can be prevented through better preparation. If student managers spend a few minutes at the start of each class taking attendance, passing out textbooks, collecting homework, or showing returning classmates what they missed, the teacher can focus on instruction. Over time, the students not only learn how to perform the roles with aplomb; they become intuitive about additional management tasks that would help the class operate more smoothly.

Freiberg described a class of 4-year-olds in one CMCD school where three students asked for a new job called the "shoelace manager." They explained that because the teacher had to help so many children tie their shoelaces before lunch, the class was frequently late to the cafeteria. They determined that the role of shoelace manager, performed by children who already knew how to loop laces, might end the delays.

"When you let kids do [these] things, it frees you up," said Pam Walton, a 6th-grade teacher at Northpoint Intermediate School in Tomball, Texas, who started using CMCD at nearby Tomball Intermediate School in 1990. "You walk down our hallways [and] it's at every door and every classroom. Kids know what to do."

GROWING PAINS

Since 1995, CMCD has expanded from three Project GRAD schools serving about 1,500 students to nearly 200 schools serving 170,000 students in the United States. CMCD also works with schools in Europe and in U.S. cities not affiliated with Project GRAD.

In the Project GRAD schools, CMCD starts by collecting data and showing faculties how to use the information to spot problems and propose solutions. In the first year after adopting CMCD, teachers and administrators attend two all-day training sessions, followed by six shorter workshops about specific components. Consistency Management specialists are available for consultation throughout the school year, and Project GRAD pays faculty advisers (one in elementary schools and four to six in middle and high schools) $1,500 annually to coach their colleagues and conduct workshops for new teachers and parents.

Freiberg, who has written or coauthored eight books and developed several collections of teaching strategies that support his work with CMCD, said it takes a few years for the recommended techniques to become routine in schools. By the 4th year of implementation in the Davis feeder system, for example, schools experienced a 74% reduction (from 1,017 to 268) in the number of discipline-related student referrals to principals (Opuni, 2001). Elementary school teachers reported in the 6th year of using CMCD that they saved an average of 44 minutes per day (4.4 school weeks) that were previously lost to disciplinary problems, while elementary teachers in the Yates High School feeder system reported saving an average of 37 minutes per day (3.7 school weeks) after 3 years of using CMCD.

Teachers in Project GRAD schools typically express appreciation for CMCD's training and techniques. In some cases, however, the demand for services initially overwhelmed both CMCD and the local Project GRAD organizations. For example, the year-round school schedule in Los Angeles and the lack of designated days for professional development prevented CMCD specialists from working with all the teachers in a building at the same time. This fragmented the training. Middle school teachers, desperate for help with classroom management, also pressured local organizers to offer CMCD training ahead of schedule. In addition, some of the CMCD consultants from Houston were not prepared to address the specific cultural needs of the California schools, said Cheryl Mabey, executive director of Project GRAD–Los Angeles.

"That whole first year I could not tell you how terrible it was," Mabey said. " The very component that is supposed to be caring, preventative, and organized is in total disarray, is doing nothing but creating havoc here."

Executive directors in Nashville and Knoxville also complained about what they considered the high cost of the program, including taking teachers and support staff off campus for CMCD training and providing gift certificates for each participant to buy instructional materials. Freiberg says the gift certificates are necessary in the first year of implementation because teachers usually pay for classroom supplies out of their own pockets or don't obtain them at all, which minimizes the impact of the designated reforms.

As for the price of the program, the average annual cost of implementing CMCD represents about 19% of Project GRAD's annual per-pupil expense, compared to 22% of the per-pupil cost for Success for All Reading and 21% for MOVE IT Math. Typically, schools pay for Consistency Management with federal grants designed to improve the educational climate, such as the Safe Schools/Healthy Schools initiative. In other cases, they use money obtained through Project GRAD's fund-raising.

Freiberg and Project GRAD leaders acknowledge some problems with the initial expansion of CMCD, including being unable to train thoroughly enough national consultants to keep up with the demand for the program. In response, they began building the capacity of the local organizations to serve the schools within their jurisdictions. CMCD coaches the school staffs, conducts a yearly Walk-About™, and reports the annual data collection, then turns supervision and training over to the local Project GRAD organization in the third year.

In part because of complaints from some high school teachers that the CMCD techniques were too "babyish" for teenagers, Freiberg also upgraded the secondary school materials. For example, to ensure that students get equal opportunities to contribute during class and stay on task, CMCD typically encourages teachers to place their names on Popsicle sticks and pull the sticks randomly from a "go-around cup" when seeking comments during class discussions. A newer option suggests using color-coded index cards printed with students' names.

On one level, it's not surprising that some teachers have resisted Consistency Management's techniques. High school teachers in particular tend to be skeptical of instructional changes because they work in large campuses that are not conducive to collaboration. They also consider themselves subject specialists who are more like college instructors than elementary and middle school teachers. Yet the teachers' reluctance to adopt new practices can cause teachers to underestimate how much meaning teenagers attach to dependable jobs and academic reinforcement—such as sending postcards to parents praising their children's accomplishments in school—when they don't ordinarily receive accolades. Consider how a recent Davis High School graduate who was accepted at an Ivy League university viewed CMCD's impact at his school. The teenager said he believes Consistency Management helped improve the culture of learning at his former high school. "Most of the students were saying, 'Okay, now I have responsibility,'" he explained. "I remember passing out assignments, turning off the lights, just random duties. It helped the discipline. The classroom would depend on you to do something. You have the responsibility. From there it built."

Davis High School social studies teacher Emily Ellis also challenges the notion that teenagers are too old for CMCD's techniques, such as classroom managers. "There are kids who vie for those positions," she said.

By the second week of class during the 2002–03 school year, her 9th graders were handling the roles of substitute manager, paper manager, book manager, folder manager, and door manager with ease and interest. Each time Ellis shifted to a different part of a lesson, her students quietly performed the appropriate jobs with little prompting.

Ellis incorporates many other parts of Consistency Management into her lessons. She lists the class procedures and the objectives of each unit of study in her classroom, along with each day's assignment and warm-up exercise. She asks students to write for 10 minutes at the start of each class and to turn in a written reflection of the week's events as their CMCD "Exit/Reflection Ticket™" each Friday. The exit tickets give her a better understanding of the students' academic progress and give the 9th graders regular practice writing for a specific purpose.

Ellis also devotes a bulletin board to Consistency Management's "Great Wall of Ideas™," in which students post questions and observations about what they're learning. The goal is to generate enthusiasm for the curriculum, give teachers ideas for lessons, and address students' different learning styles and interests. In one of Ellis's freshman geography classes at Davis, students looked through their textbooks at the beginning of the term and noted things they were curious about. One student wrote that she "would like to learn more about the San Andreas Fault." One student said he wanted to know "why China is a communist country." Another student was perplexed by a photographic essay about inflation, which carried the title, "Money to Burn." "Why would you use the money to light your stove, even though it has little value?" she asked. Ellis planned to address those questions by working the topics into her lessons throughout the year.

Periodic visits from CMCD consultants help ensure that teachers consistently use techniques such as the Great Wall of Ideas, although not necessarily the same way. However, when teachers see consultants marking off items on a prepared checklist during a Walk-About, they assume that the observers are seeking confirmation of strict compliance instead of general evidence of sound practices.

Freiberg said CMCD offers to share the data by department, by grade level, or by individual classroom, but some schools don't provide time for faculties to review and respond to the results, which causes confusion and misconceptions about how the information will be used.

"It's not an assessment," Freiberg said. "It's truly feedback. We give a sheet ahead of time to the teacher and ask, 'What do you want us to look for?' They fill it out ahead of time and then we look at it so we can give them feedback on what they're interested in, not just what we're interested in."

Even when teachers appreciate CMCD's techniques, however, they can become lax about the practices over time and fail to provide continuity from one class to the next. As one teacher indicated in a survey cited in Kimberly Agnew's dissertation, "Keeping up with the little things is hard."

Agnew noted that teachers need ongoing "refresher" courses to understand not just what CMCD includes but how the classroom management strategies fit into a school's overall mission to improve teaching and learning. Teachers also need regular guidance about how to advance the CMCD methods beyond a basic level, she said.

To spread more of the strategies that prompted Marshall Middle School's turnaround, CMCD added a feature called Teacher Implementation Pioneers (TIP), which identifies and trains a small group of teachers before the entire faculty formally adopts CMCD. These TIP instructors become on-site experts who can demonstrate effective strategies and quickly address their colleagues' concerns. CMCD also formalized the process of including janitors, office clerks, and other staff members in training sessions so they will understand the recommended practices and use them with students.

"We're trying to build the climate for this in secondary schools," said one CMCD official. "It's very rare to have teachers doing the same thing consistently throughout the building. Most of the time they're isolated and using different programs and models. They're not working together as a whole school."

At Marshall Middle School, most teachers still use Consistency Management nearly a decade later, although implementation levels have declined from a high of 90% in 1998–99 to 79% in 2000–01, the latest year for which statistics are available (Opuni & Ochoa, 2002a).

In the fall of 2002, 7th-grade reading teacher Angela Raines apologized to a visitor for not having selected classroom managers by the third week of school. Other requirements had gotten in the way, she said, but she planned to select student managers that week. When an office aide came to the door and asked for the class lunch list, Raines had to interrupt a discussion about the role of the protagonist in short stories.

"Do you see why we need managers?" Raines asked her students, smiling. "So I could have had a nice, handsome face to greet people as they come to the door. We need to work on that."

At the end of class that day, she collected "employment" applications from the students, many of them immigrants whose first language is not English.

"Miss," one girl asked her, "what does it mean by qualification?"

It means "have you done this before," Raines explained. "What skills do you have that relate to this position?"

One student wrote on his application for substitute manager that he would be responsible for explaining the classroom procedures to temporary teachers. "I haven't been a substitute manager but I am here all the time," he wrote. "I want to apply for this 'cause I see other people do it."

Another student said his skills would be well suited to the job of door manager. "I can move fast expecialy [sic] with my hands," he wrote.

Two students expressed interest in the position of class manager. One wrote that his "skills are to get the class quiet and to pass out papers and to greet people when they come through the door." The other noted that "I'm while [sic] behaved and I have a good mimerey [sic]. I'm good with people and I'm pelight [sic]."

In her 6 years at Marshall, Raines said, she has found that CMCD "really, really works" to improve the school climate. Most students choose to be managers and learn valuable skills from the jobs. "A lot of the kids who would be behavior problems take these jobs and don't misbehave. They look forward to it and take pride in it. You never have to say to a child, 'You didn't do this [job] this morning.' They come right in and pass out folders or whatever it is. Then I don't have fifteen kids reaching and grabbing for things in the back of the room."

Although the jobs are voluntary, Raines said she sometimes encourages reluctant students to apply for certain positions if she thinks they need a self-esteem boost or a positive reminder of the right way to behave.

"I've seen some of the worst students turn around" by becoming CMCD managers, she said. "I think it's because they have something to look forward to and have ownership of the classroom. . . . It teaches them responsibility and leadership. It gives them pride in themselves. They want to do well."

Chapter 6

CONCENTRATING ON
TEACHING AND LEARNING

If positive reinforcements were all that students needed to succeed, the children in Project GRAD elementary schools would sail through to college. Colorful wall charts, inspirational posters, and photographs of smiling students splash the walls. Bookcases overflow with literature. Amusing props, hand puppets, and cozy reading rugs seem to sweep away the distinctions between the playhouse and the schoolhouse.

The classrooms are stimulating and inviting, adjectives that people rarely associate with urban elementary schools. More importantly, they are consistent. For 90 uninterrupted minutes a day, everyone in a Project GRAD elementary school focuses on Success for All (SFA), an international reading program that combines phonemic awareness (how the sounds in words work), decoding skills (identifying and connecting syllables, rhymes, and other parts of spoken language in print), and regular assessments of children's progress.

Success for All relies on sequential lessons developed by specialists outside the schools—with scripts to follow and instruction timed down to the minute—to ensure that teachers and students stay on task. The format is designed to eliminate uncertainty about the progression of the curriculum and the methods likely to increase student achievement.

With Success for All, every teacher uses the same hand signals and phrases, and all posters, books, videotapes, puppets, and lesson plans come from the company. Teachers are supposed to post daily and weekly objectives in the classroom. Students who fall behind receive 20 minutes a day of one-on-one tutoring in addition to the regular reading instruction and may receive other assistance as recommended by an SFA family support team.

A school using SFA formally assesses students' progress every 8 weeks. Teachers separate students by reading ability, but children can switch groups frequently throughout the school year depending on their progress. All certified teachers in the school, from the librarian to the regular classroom instructor, work with a group of students during the 90-minute reading block to keep class sizes small.

Such precision represents both the beauty and the banality of Project GRAD's reading program: It ensures that all children progress toward mastery of basic skills, but can also stifle the most creative teachers and the most advanced students.

"We know that the teachers in urban schools are all over the place," said Dr. Robert E. Slavin, who in 1987 cofounded Success for All at Johns Hopkins University. "Some of the best you've seen in your life are there. You'll see better ones than in suburban schools. But the bottom end is much worse than the bottom ones in suburban schools. And you've got to have something that's not insulting to the most outstanding teachers and yet well enough laid out that a teacher who's really struggling can succeed. That's a fundamental difficulty in the design of reform models with high-poverty schools."

In addition to SFA, Project GRAD elementary schools also spend 90 minutes a day on math.[1] Most of the schools follow the MOVE IT Math curriculum, which emphasizes the seven building blocks of math literacy identified by the National Council of Teachers of Mathematics standards. These include problem solving; patterns, relations, and functions; numbers and numeration; operations and computation; measurement; geometry; and probability, statistics, and graphing. MOVE IT Math uses children's literature and science to provide a context for math, makes connections to children's past experiences, and involves students in hands-on explorations of mathematical concepts.

Ironically, MOVE IT Math started out as a looser configuration of objectives and activities. But after teachers complained that the program wasn't fully aligned to state standards and didn't have structured lesson plans, Project GRAD made MOVE IT Math more specific and sequential.

The original MOVE IT Math program focused on "the big ideas of math. Then it was up to the teacher to figure out how to fit it into what they were doing," said Ann Stiles, math manager for Project GRAD–USA.

"That was expecting too much of a classroom teacher. There isn't enough time in the day to fit reform into the regular work of classroom teachers without support."

One of the early lessons for Project GRAD was how much ongoing training most teachers require before they can effectively transfer curriculum, whether it's prescriptive or just descriptive. That's because, appearances aside, positive reinforcements are *not* all that students need to succeed. They also must have challenging instruction from skilled teachers. And without targeted interventions, students in impoverished schools are the least likely to get the right assistance (Lippman et al., 1996). Their schools have the greatest difficulty hiring qualified teachers, finding substitutes for frequently absent teachers, and providing adequate classroom resources. A Teach for America study conducted by Raymond, Fletcher, and Luque (as cited in Darling-Hammond & Youngs, 2002) found that during the 1999–2000 school year, about half of Houston's new teachers lacked certification and 35% didn't have a bachelor's degree.

Controlling the variable of teacher quality, therefore, becomes one of the most formidable challenges for Project GRAD or any urban school reform initiative. It's not enough to expect schools to hire only teachers who have demonstrated success in the classroom. There simply aren't sufficient numbers of excellent instructors to fill all the positions, particularly educators who know how to reach students with limited English proficiency or learning disabilities (Alexander, Heaviside, & Farris, 1999). Nor can the schools adopt a new curriculum or different instructional approaches and expect every teacher to apply them with skill and confidence. It can take years for teachers, with the best intentions and the right support, to change the content of their lessons and the techniques they use to convey them.

New teachers, in particular, suffer from professional neglect. In a recent study of four large U.S. states by researchers at the Harvard Graduate School of Education, only 44% of new teachers reported that extra assistance was available to them, and about half of the new teachers went through the entire first year without being observed by a more experienced educator (Kardos, 2003). Studies show that 40 to 50% of teachers leave at the end of 5 years (Keller, 2003). Schools serving a high percentage of poor children lose 20% of their teachers each year on average, virtually ensuring continual turnover in buildings that most need stability.

Given those realities, Project GRAD decided to work closely with the schools' existing staffs, providing intensive training in both subject content and teaching methods instead of leaving learning to chance. Each school must designate a full-time staff member to coordinate the Success for All reading program, organize tutoring sessions, and coach their colleagues. In addition, Project GRAD sends reading and math specialists to each school several times a week so they can observe instruction, model lessons, and track down resources for teachers. (Project GRAD assigns a full-time math coach to some struggling schools. Through school district initiatives in Atlanta and Los Angeles, full-time math coaches work in all the elementary schools there.) Finally, national consultants visit the schools several times a year to conduct structured classroom observations, which are announced in advance, and provide brief updates of each teacher's progress using the programs.

For example, in March 2002 national consultants from Success for All came calling on Sherman Elementary School in Houston. It was their second scheduled visit of the school term. The two consultants, along with members of Sherman's administrative team and support staff from Project GRAD–Houston, circulated throughout the building to observe reading instruction during the 90-minute period. Each individual session was intended to provide a "camera glimpse" of the classroom, which the consultants would use when offering feedback to the staff.

One observation team started out with a group of children reading at a 1st-grade level. The middle-aged teacher sat in a rocking chair and held up a copy of the book, *Bored—Nothing to Do*, while the students gathered around her on a rug. Loudly and emphatically, the teacher read each word in a theatrical voice that adults sometimes use when they're trying to create excitement for children, but which ends up sounding false.

"A *lot* of *words* to *recognize, too!*" she announced to the children as the SFA consultant, Sherman's assistant principal, and a Project GRAD reading specialist crouched in tiny chairs at the back of the classroom. "I *love* the way the person that drew the pictures, the *illustrator*, I *love* what he did. What was the illustrator's name? Remember what I told you—if we don't see the illustrator's name, if it's not listed on the book, *usually*—can I see all eyes up here?—*usually* it is the one who wrote the book."

About 5 minutes after they had entered the classroom and made notations on a preprinted form, the observers quietly walked out to the hallway and discussed what they had seen. They agreed that the teacher did not have a firm command of the SFA-recommended techniques, such as Think-Pair-Share, which encourages students first to mentally consider a point about the book, then share their thoughts with a partner before returning to the teacher's main lesson.

Assistant principal Martha Medina said that the teacher, a long-term substitute who had started working at Sherman just 2 months before, was one of five new teachers on the staff. She had missed participating in the SFA workshops that the other instructors had attended at the beginning of the school year.

"So what can we do? What are some things we can suggest to her?" prompted Marisol Hernandez, one of the SFA consultants.

"Can we do a model lesson?" Medina suggested.

Yes, Hernandez agreed, demonstrations from experienced reading instructors would help, as would spending at least 2 days observing exemplary teachers leading classes on similar reading levels. The new teacher must learn to ask questions that will help students think about what they're reading.

In the next classroom, the observers watched a group of bilingual children reading at a 1st-grade level, and the differences from the previous classroom were immediately clear. In this class, the young Spanish-speaking teacher wrote a few vocabulary words associated with the book *La Señorita Runfio* on the board, then he randomly pulled sticks printed with students' names from a plastic cup and asked the children questions about the book's characters and plot. Next, the children read the paperback book aloud, moving their fingers across the words on each page. As the children read, the teacher circulated and listened to each student in turn, stopping occasionally to assist those who were struggling with pronunciation. While the teacher moved around the room, so did Hernandez, who also speaks Spanish. She noted the sound recognition and decoding strategies the students used and simultaneously scanned the classroom for evidence of the SFA-recommended displays, such as a large Word Wall listing the vocabulary words studied during the week.

After a few minutes, the teacher checked the SFA guidebook for instructions. He then asked the children to stop reading and to observe him as he held up a laminated square printed with the capital letter *g*. He prompted them to jointly sound out the letter phonetically, practice writing it with their index fingers in the air, then identify a few short words in which the letter *g* appeared.

"He's doing a wonderful job," Hernandez said when the observers left the classroom. "He's modeling for the children. When I walked over to listen, they were all following the reading. They went on to letter formation, and the children got to move around a lot. All of the skills they're learning are transferable to English."

The observers moved around the school throughout the morning, watching the guided partner reading in one classroom, nodding as children made good predictions about plot development in another classroom, and noting the oral language development in yet another room. "His class made a big jump from the last time I tested," Hernandez said about one teacher.

"She's putting them into the story," the consultant observed after leaving another classroom. "She's asking them what their partner said to get everyone involved in finding answers."

"They're learning, but not to their potential," Hernandez noted after watching another teacher. "You have to gradually release the responsibility to the children."

Every classroom at Sherman had related activities and contained similar stacks of books, samples of student writing, and colorful props. Yet each classroom also differed, too, owing to the teachers' preferences and styles. The job of the consultants was to figure out how much variation was necessary to accommodate each teacher's interests and strengths and how much consistency was essential to ensure that every student learned to read well.

The implementation visit is not intended "to be an evaluation but to see where you are in the change process and how you're using the lessons," Hernandez said. "They've done a wonderful job here at Sherman. They have real strong leadership."

The observers visited each teacher at least twice throughout the day, moving in and out the classrooms at various points during the period so they would have a fuller understanding of how the lessons developed over time. On the forms, the consultants occasionally annotated their observations to explain what each teacher was doing right. Hernandez noted that some teachers got the children to interact with the text, showed them how to diagram a sentence, provided time for practice, activated their prior knowledge of the topic, and asked analytical questions to help students synthesize literature, not just memorize the plots.

In one classroom, the observers watched as a formerly struggling teacher demonstrated a solid lesson that engaged and delighted the children. Sherman's administrators had prompted the turnaround by reducing the number of students in the class and providing additional training in the SFA techniques.

On this day, the teacher first led the students through a recorded song that encouraged them to act out the letters of the alphabet ("J, juggling jellybeans . . . L, looking like lions") then to form each of the letters with their fingers in the air. To make connections between the verbal and written forms of language, the teacher next used a series of activities to focus on the letter of the day—*w*. The children practiced saying "Wuh, wuh, wuh," the sound that the letter *w* makes, then repeated some words in which the letter *w* appears: what, which, where, and why. With an Alphie the Alligator puppet on her hand, the teacher reached into a plastic bin and pulled out some laminated pictures of words starting with the letter *w*. The children correctly identified the watermelon and the wagon, but had more difficulty with the wishing well. "She forgot with the first two [words] to emphasize the phonetic sounds, but remembered to do that with the third," Hernandez said afterward. "She's really trying."

At the end of the observations, the consultants conducted a detailed debriefing with Sherman's administrative team. They praised the principal and assistant principal for their leadership, saying they had seen improvements in the quality of teaching since their last visit to the school several months before. Teachers seemed more confident with the lessons, they said, and weren't as nervous having visitors in the classroom. They were integrating reading and writing, using graphics to show students how to visually organize their ideas for writing, and following the sequence of lessons recommended by SFA. In addition, they said, Sherman had enlisted parents' support in helping students read at home and volunteering as tutors at school.

Nevertheless, the consultants pointed out that many teachers were still at a basic level with SFA. This was not surprising, given that some were new to the building and to the program. But after 7 years as an SFA school, Sherman had not performed quite as well as expected. While the rate of non–special education students passing the state reading exam had risen from 61% before the school became part of Project GRAD to 78% by 2002, Sherman remained second lowest among the Davis feeder schools (Opuni & Ochoa, 2002b). Passing rates on the state reading exam for schools with similar demographics were 10 to 20 percentage points higher. In another sign of inconsistency, Sherman students who performed at or above grade level in reading on national standardized tests jumped from 35% during the 1997–98 school year to 71% in 2001–02 on the Aprenda Test, but inexplicably dropped from 42% to 34% on the Stanford-9 Test during the same period.

Researchers noted similar reversals in the Stanford-9 Test results at other Project GRAD schools and in the Houston Independent School District as a whole during the same period (Opuni & Ochoa, 2002b). They considered several possible reasons for the declines, including the misalignment of the district's curriculum with the Stanford-9 Test questions and the district's policy of testing all students, regardless of their proficiency with English.

Hernandez had another explanation for Sherman's results. The teachers "have all the mechanics of the program in place," she said, "but they need to move to the next level."

For example, many students were able to decode the words on a page but they did not comprehend what they were reading. An SFA consultant suggested that teachers model more techniques for thinking about text passages, showing students how skilled readers make sense of the words on a page by using context clues or mental imagery. She also recommended that teachers do a better job of integrating SFA's weekly objectives—such as understanding the difference between fact and opinion—by weaving the main ideas throughout each day's activities. Hernandez then gave Sherman's administrators short scripts that teachers could use during Think-Alouds, a strategy for verbally analyzing the meaning of a particular passage.

The explicit directions are part of how Success for All aims to take the guesswork out of instruction so that all children can read fluently by the time they leave 3rd grade. Yet Robert Slavin acknowledges that Success for All does not succeed with every student. As with any packaged curriculum, he said, SFA depends on cooperation from teachers and administrators.

"In big cities where Project GRAD works and where we mostly work, schools don't make free and open choices that often," Slavin said in an interview. "Even when they have a vote [about participating in SFA], they don't feel like they have a choice. We try to make sure it's not imposed on them, but there may be things like the principal says, 'I really want to do this and the district wants me to do it and if you don't vote for this, we might have to do something else that you won't like as much.'"

Like Project GRAD, Success for All has grown rapidly in the past decade. By 2002, the reading program had spread to more than 1,800 schools serving about 1 million students in the United States and in several other countries. Schools using SFA overwhelmingly serve high-poverty populations (Slavin & Madden, 2001), both because they are the ones most likely to need a major overhaul of their reading programs and because they can use federal grants to pay for Success for All, which runs about $70,000 per school in the first year and $25,000 a year thereafter (Lemann, 1998).

SFA has developed reading components from preschool through 8th grade, including adaptations for English as a Second Language instruction and extensions in mathematics, science, and social studies. Most SFA schools have posted significant gains on standardized tests, with the greatest progress occurring among African-American and Latino students (Slavin & Madden, 1999). In 1998, the American Federation of Teachers (1998a) reviewed 250 studies of reading and English language arts programs used nationwide and cited SFA as one of the seven most promising approaches for raising academic achievement, especially for struggling students.

"Because this program was developed for, and is primarily used by, high-poverty Title I schools, some have the idea that the program is primarily remedial," the American Federation of Teachers report concluded. "The truth, however, is that SFA's developers went out of their way to strike a workable balance between challenging content and the acquisition of basic skills, incorporating everything from guided skill instruction to basals to children's classics such as *Charlotte's Web*."

In 2002 the Center for Research on the Education of Students Placed at Risk (CRESPAR) concluded that Success for All was one of only 3 out of 29 school-wide improvement programs that had demonstrated the "strongest evidence of effectiveness" (Borman et al., 2002). Another study, which examined the impact and cost of Success for All, concluded that students in the program "complete eighth grade at a younger age, with better achievement outcomes, fewer special education placements, and less frequent retentions in grade" compared to those in traditional remedial education classes (Borman & Hewes, 2003).

Yet SFA has critics, too. For example, Stanley Pogrow (2002), associate professor of education at the University of Arizona at Tucson, has written several articles disputing the student achievement gains in Success for All schools. In addition, researchers Steven Ross, Lana Smith, and Jason Casey (as cited in Groff, 2003) reported that SFA benefited students in only half the school districts they examined.

Some teachers who have used SFA question the need for so much documentation of students' progress and so many prescriptive lesson plans. They resent what they consider the program's "cookie-cutter" approach to teaching, which they believe hinders an instructor's freedom to adapt lessons to students' needs and interests.

"It's extremely time-consuming. The paperwork is enormous," a teacher from Colorado complained about SFA (Hill, 1998). "It's a very formal, rigid program." However, the teacher also conceded that SFA "has more positive aspects than negative aspects. It's an effective program, especially if you have good teachers. But any program is going to work pretty well if you've got good teachers. I think we could present a good reading program without the structure, rigidity, and bookkeeping that comes with Success for All."

A teacher at Sherman Elementary School expressed similar reservations about SFA. She said she considers it "a good program. It just gets tiresome for the kids and the teachers. It's the same exact thing every single day. You have a rigorous schedule to follow—ten minutes for this and fifteen minutes for that. I don't think they want you to deviate from that. They give you a script for it.

"As a new teacher, for the first semester, it's good. But after that, as you know your kids, you want to have more freedom."

The teacher said she appreciates the training that Project GRAD provides for SFA and MOVE IT Math. Having specialists on campus to model lessons and being able to observe colleagues in their classrooms definitely helps, she said. But she doesn't believe it's necessary to put every classroom under regular surveillance.

The frequent observations "kind of take the fun out of teaching," she said. "Even my kids would say, 'Again?'" Visitors appear so often that "I feel like I have to put on a show. I know I shouldn't, but I do. I bribe my kids so they'll pay attention to me when people are in the room instead of looking around. I say, 'If you're on your best behavior, I'll give you cupcakes.' It works most of the time."

In an interview, Slavin responded to criticisms of SFA in different ways. Regarding Pogrow's attacks against SFA, Slavin said the researcher's claims have become increasingly "bizarre," part of what he believes is a vendetta to discredit the organization. "I don't know what else you can possibly do," Slavin said. "This is the most extensively researched program in history . . . and yet he still says it doesn't work. It's a lie."

Slavin takes the teachers' concerns more seriously, however, and he has addressed many of the complaints by adapting SFA. Project GRAD has helped, he said, by demonstrating the importance of having a local organization to support schools and provide consistent and frequent contact to educators.

"One of the things that's been important to the effectiveness of Project GRAD is that they have a staff locally who are able to be in the schools a lot more often than we are. There's more follow-up and ability to know the local context," Slavin said. "Project GRAD has influenced our thinking so that we're evolving in a similar direction to do more concentrated work and [provide] more flexible kind of assistance on the ground to schools."

For example, instead of sending two-person teams for 2 days twice a year to observe schools, SFA has begun placing more local specialists in schools for shorter visits but on a more regular basis. In addition, Slavin said, SFA's trainers are trying to set up stronger partnerships with schools, focusing on problem solving instead of verifying compliance.

"We wanted to move the focus to more looking at children's performance and the school's use of data, the guts of what the lesson is about rather than the exact times and sequences," he said. "So one school might say we're having problems with classroom management. Another might say we're having difficulty with English language learners, and another with higher-order thinking skills. We would, while attending to the basics, have a particular focus on those goals and set up benchmarks with the things that the schools are trying to change."

The criticism about SFA's structure and rigidity notwithstanding, schools serving impoverished students can tolerate a lower margin of error than schools whose students come from homes with print-rich environments where well-educated parents read to them and monitor their progress. With high turnover rates among students and teachers always threatening to sever the strong relationships that make high achievement possible, urban schools must be more intentional about the educational foundation that children receive. At all grade levels, very little learning occurs when students can't read. At least one state projects future prison construction based on the number of 2nd graders who don't know how to read (Chase, 2000).

The instructional consistency that SFA provides also contrasts with the typical hodgepodge of activities in urban schools, which have suffered through so many quick-fix solutions for chronic low achievement that nothing really changes. At the same time, if earnest teachers haven't found a comfortable balance between the formulaic parts of Success for All and the flexibility they desire as practitioners, then the professional coaching they received either wasn't adequate or failed to take into account their particular needs.

In Houston, after many years of using Success for All, some educators at the school and district level have questioned whether it is the most effective reading program available for disadvantaged students. Conflicts erupted when the staffs at several schools within Project GRAD feeder systems wanted to use a reading curriculum developed by the Rodeo Institute for Teacher Excellence (RITE) in Texas instead of Success for All. Robert Stockwell, chief academic officer for HISD, said officials agreed with Project GRAD that it was better to maintain consistency within the feeder systems by sticking with one reading program.

But to former Houston school board member Don McAdams, Project GRAD's loyalty to Success for All suggests that the organization might be developing a bureaucratic resistance to change. "I still believe that, strategically, it [Project GRAD] is sound and well managed," McAdams said, but he faulted the organization's leaders for not being "as open as they need to be to continuous improvement, to finding the best in the market and using it. . . . Maybe they're not holding up Success for All to as intense scrutiny as it needs to be because they've got so much invested in it."

Project GRAD–Houston extended its support for reading through the middle grades beginning in the 2001–02 school year; 6th, 7th, and 8th graders who still read below a 6th-grade level receive 90 to 110 minutes a day—the equivalent of a double class period—of Success for All until they progress. Theoretically, students shouldn't need this extra assistance if Success for All worked well at the elementary level.

Dr. Laurie Ballering, director of middle school programs for Project GRAD–Houston, said schools that have implemented SFA well send very few struggling readers to the 6th grade. Reading intervention in the middle grades rarely becomes necessary for students in the Davis feeder system, for example, but more typically occurs for those in the Wheatley and Yates feeder systems.

COUNTING ON THE POWER OF MATH

Ninety-seven percent of the children at Lamar Elementary School[2] qualify for free- and reduced-price lunches, the federal standard for poverty. Seven percent of the students have identified learning disabilities, and about half speak only limited English. More than one fourth of Lamar's 300 students move during the school year, including the children at a nearby homeless shelter, which means that teachers always have a steady stream of new students to acclimate.

Nevertheless, Lamar is rich with the educational qualities that count in a school. Students' artwork and essays cover the hallways and classroom bulletin boards. Stacks of new books and supplies fill the bookcases and storage rooms. Classrooms are orderly yet animated. Teachers and students speak respectfully to each other. There is a happy buzz that extends from the office to the cafeteria and to every classroom in between.

Barry Morris, comptroller for the Greater Houston Community Foundation, said that Lamar was always one of his favorite schools to visit when he worked as director of finance for Project GRAD. However, he didn't realize how unusual Lamar was for an urban school until he toured classrooms in another city that wanted to become part of Project GRAD.

"I would visit Lamar Elementary and see that the halls were clean and everything was orderly and kids and teachers were happy," he said. By contrast, an elementary school that he visited in the other city was chaotic. "I walked into that school, a really nice brick building, and I got inside and kids were yelling in the halls, teachers were screaming at kids. This one kindergarten teacher was just screaming at the top of her lungs. It was just stunning. I was shaken. I was walking through classrooms where teachers were trying to teach and kids were all over the place. It was an unbelievable experience. I thought, 'Man, maybe Houston is doing something right.'"

Lamar has received an exemplary rating from the Texas Education Agency, which means that at least 90% of the students have passed the annual state exams in reading, writing, and math. Indeed, it's one of the rare urban schools where the students' high achievement levels actually surpass their high rate of poverty. Ninety-nine percent of Lamar's non–special education students passed the state math exams during the 2001–02 school year—the highest rate in the Davis feeder system—up from 38% of the students who did so in 1994, the first year of Project GRAD (Opuni & Ochoa, 2002b). In addition, 97% of Lamar's students passed the state reading exams, up from 79% in 1994. Most significantly, Lamar's 5th graders, most of whom have been in the Project GRAD program since they started school, now perform at comparable rates in math and reading as their peers in Houston and the state of Texas. Sixty-five percent of Lamar's students scored at or above grade level in math on the Stanford-9 national standardized exam in 2001–02, compared to 26% of the students who did so in the 1997–98 school year.

"One thing we know is that those who have maintained a reasonable critical mass of implementation [of the Project GRAD components] have always seen very solid results," said Kwame A. Opuni, the evaluator from the University of St. Thomas in Houston, who has tracked Lamar's progress along with other Project GRAD sites. "It's just like where we started at Lamar. If you look at the first reports I wrote, it wasn't at the top. When they hired a new principal, they hired a [former] teacher at the same school who had been through all the training, and right from the first year they've been at the top."

Principal Alma Lara, who earns excellent ratings for leadership in Project GRAD–Houston's internal evaluation of program implementation, tries to maintain Lamar's progress by making sure the curriculum is consistent and that teachers are uniformly capable of following it. She noted that students who have little regularity in their lives need structure and dependable routines.

One of the major ways Lara monitors the school's performance is by observing teachers and examining test scores for evidence of their effectiveness. During one walk-through accompanied by several consultants and visitors, Lara found many examples of the staff's ability to use MOVE IT Math's strategies.

In a 4th-grade bilingual class that she observed, the teacher presented a lesson about capacity. Working in groups of five, the students first examined a variety of plastic containers, trying to determine how much the containers could hold of assorted solids and liquids. This process enabled them to see and touch mathematical concepts, such as volume, while sharpening their estimation skills. To reinforce the mathematical terms under review, the teacher also wrote key words in both English and Spanish on an overhead projector:

Capacity = Capacidad
Gallon = Galón
Pint = Pinta

The teacher integrated Consistency Management concepts into the lesson as well. All of the children had laminated signs at their places, indicating their roles in the group. One child acted as the recorder, to keep track of information; one served as the facilitator, to encourage everyone's participation; one performed the role of timekeeper, to keep all the students on task; one acted as the maintenance director, to make sure everyone had the right supplies; and one served as the reporter, writing down the group's responses.

During the observers' visit to a 5th-grade classroom, the students were engaged in solving geometric problems. Working in small groups, they used plastic Peg-Boards and rubber bands to physically display various shapes, then wrote about their findings in notebooks.

On the overhead projector, the teacher had listed a practical problem, the type typically found on the state's annual math exams: Celeste had a small garden in her backyard. Her garden was 6 yards long and 5 yards wide. She wanted to use 1/5 of her garden to plant green beans. How many *square feet* did Celeste use to plant her green beans? What is the area of the rest of her garden in feet squared?

Below the problem were the steps the teacher expected her students to follow in their investigations:

1. Understanding
2. Strategy
3. Work operation
4. Write about your process.

As the children discussed the concepts at their tables, the teacher walked around the room, checking the students' work and encouraging further inquiries.

"Now," she said to one group of students, "do you think the area of your short, long rectangles are going to be the same area as the others?"

At other tables, children seemed eager to challenge themselves instead of settling for easy answers or copying each other's work.

"How did Robert do that?" one child asked out loud, looking at the geometric pattern that his friend had displayed on a Peg-Board.

Rather than wait for the teacher or his classmates to explain, the boy tried to figure out the application by himself. His face wrinkled in concentration, he manipulated the rubber bands on his Peg-Board for a few minutes, then his face broke into a grin. "Oh, I got it now. Hallelujah! I think I got it. There it is—a tetragon," he said, proudly displaying his product in the air.

In another classroom, 3rd graders used colorful cutout shapes to study fractions. The playful nature of the lesson belied its serious focus on mathematical modeling and understanding. By investigating why certain techniques work, testing new theories, revising thinking, and discovering relationships among numbers and patterns, students develop the capacity to communicate as mathematicians (Romberg, 2002).

"Tell me what happens when you add two one-sixteenths," the teacher said.

Several students called out the answer.

"Okay, prove it," the teacher said, smiling. "Show me."

The students held up the shape of "1/8."

"That's right," she said, pleased. "Now you've proven the answer. Very good. Now look at the activity on your worksheet. You and you partners work together."

Excited students leaned across or jumped around the tables, putting laminated shapes together to help them solve a series of problems that combined fractions and basic algebraic principles. For example: $1/3 = x/12$.

"I think it will be four because three times four equals twelve," one little girl said to her partner, confidently recalling her prior knowledge of multiplication tables and applying it to a new situation. Each girl used the laminated fraction pieces to verify the hunch.

"Oh," a girl at a nearby table said, flush with another discovery. "I wonder if that's a fraction family."

Standing back and watching the activity, the teacher beamed. "I just love hearing those little conversations and discoveries," she said. "It would be so hard to teach them that, but when they figure it out on their own, it's wonderful."

After the brief tour, Lara said she was pleased with the results. She saw many examples of teachers challenging students to think deeply about math and make connections between problems and past experiences. In most classrooms, teachers were using the MOVE IT Math lessons and the provided materials. Students were comfortable with the routines and could follow them with minimal direction. They used the language of math when solving problems and writing about them. In addition, in all the classrooms there was extensive evidence of math applications, including examples of students' work posted on bulletin boards.

"It's a struggle" to keep the school's test scores high, Lara acknowledged, but MOVE IT Math makes it easier. "Kids have many problems. But we say that's not an excuse. We spend more time on instruction. We provide after-school and Saturday tutoring. We just have high expectations that they can learn."

Lara grew up in the neighborhood where her students live. When her own family arrived in the United States from Mexico, she was 9 years old, the second oldest of what would eventually be 11 children. Her father died when she was 12 and her mother was ill, so Lara and her siblings depended on their teachers for more than learning a new language.

"Teachers would come with boxes and bags of groceries to our house," she said. "It changed the way I thought about teachers."

After graduating from Davis High School, Lara became the first in her family to attend a university. She received several scholarships, including one from a Davis alumni group and one from a neighborhood community center that had become her second home.

In 1976, straight out of college and newly married, Lara took a job teaching at Lamar. After 2 years, she grew frustrated that so many of her students weren't ready for 2nd grade, so she decided to move to the 1st grade and change things. She later became a curriculum writer for the school district, but subsequently returned to Lamar as a teacher and then a guidance counselor. After a short stint as a parent involvement specialist at the district level, she became Lamar's principal in 1997.

Lara embraced Project GRAD from the start, believing that something drastic needed to happen in the Davis feeder system to help the schools advance. More importantly, she said, Project GRAD helped change the culture of the community's schools from resigned to resolute.

"The commitment from some of the teachers, the expectations for the children to achieve, it just wasn't there," Lara said of the period before Project GRAD. "You know, they thought, 'These kids are poor. What do you expect?'

"We would make all sorts of excuses why they weren't succeeding. Even me, having come out of that [same environment], I used to say, 'Well, we just can't expect them to do well on an English test. They learned Spanish first.' And then I started listening to myself and I was like, 'What am I saying?' If somebody had that expectation of me, I wouldn't have made it."

Lara said she also realized that if she wanted the teachers at Lamar to set high expectations for the students, she had to set high expectations for the teachers. As principal, she had to do everything possible to make sure the faculty succeeded, whether that meant providing substitutes so teachers could observe successful colleagues, paying for additional training, or setting up tutoring for struggling students. Likewise, she had to set a high standard for her own leadership: "It's not just, I hold *you* accountable. You hold *me* accountable. It's a two-way thing," she said.

Lamar's faculty members chose to lengthen the school day Monday through Thursday and dismiss early on Friday afternoons so they could have time for staff development each week. By modifying the school calendar—students attend from 7:45 a.m. to 3:15 p.m. Monday through Thursday and half days on Fridays—Lamar freed up 2 hours a week to use for staff training. Some days, teachers examine students' work and tests, looking for learning gaps and solutions. Other days, they read and discuss articles and books about education. Teachers have also used the time to take college classes.

One of the reasons Lamar's math scores are so high, Lara said, is that MOVE IT Math shows students how concepts work in the real world. They don't just memorize facts; they use what they learn. Instead of staring in confusion at a basic algebra problem, for example, children in elementary grades learn how to balance equations by using a scale and weights or manipulating different-sized blocks to understand proportionality.

"This morning, I saw a fifth grade class and the teacher was doing something like four raised to the fourth power plus three to the third power plus some other figure, and I thought, 'Oh, my gosh, ten-year-olds are learning algebra,'" Lara said.

Actually, the foundations of algebra start in preschool, when teachers begin building students' understanding of the concept of equality. Using balance beams and other tools, students learn that the equal sign in mathematics means that the sums on either side are proportionate. Similarly, young children use two- and three-unit blocks to make sense of place value and trading.

Like Success for All, MOVE IT Math recommends that teachers follow a prescribed daily sequence of activities that includes 5 minutes for homework, 5 minutes for a warm-up exercise, 10 to 15 minutes for problem solving, 30 to 45 minutes for the focus lesson, 20 to 25 minutes for exploratory centers, and 5 minutes for reflection. The total time spent on math each day far surpasses what schools did before, which might account for some of the students' achievement gains.

"This is my second time teaching 2nd grade. My students have been extremely successful in math this year," a teacher from the Wheatley feeder system wrote in an anonymous evaluation of MOVE IT Math (Opuni, 2001). "They can do long division, and multiple-digit multiplication. They far exceed any class I've ever taught due to the move it math [sic] strategies."

"My students made outstanding progress by using the program," said another teacher from the Wheatley feeder system. "The use of the skip counting made division and multiplication more enjoyable and successful."

The supports that MOVE IT Math currently provides to schools were not available in 1994 when Project GRAD began using the program, however.

MOVE IT Math was the first Project GRAD curriculum that the elementary schools in the Davis feeder system chose to implement. Teachers from the Davis, Wheatley, and Yates feeder systems all struggled with the math concepts at first, and many instructors suggested improvements, citing in particular the need for more demonstration lessons and lesson-planning strategies.

"Write a curriculum that smoothly introduces, builds, and transfers these scattered ideas into a usable teaching plan that is orderly and sequential," one teacher wrote in an evaluation (Opuni, 2001).

"Too many resources to pull from," another teacher wrote. "Doesn't tell us how to teach the lesson."

And in a reference to the conflict between teachers who want more directions and teachers who want less, one educator wrote that the "curriculum is not flexible and teachers are not allowed to use their own judgment to plan the sequence of lessons."

Unlike Success for All, MOVE IT Math has not been the subject of extensive educational research. That troubles Uri Treisman, the University of Texas math professor who directs the Charles A. Dana Center. Treisman said he has spent time in Project GRAD's classrooms and found the math instruction simplistic and shallow, with students unable to recall basic math facts.

"I don't know anyone who has looked at MOVE IT Math who was impressed," Treisman said. "Project GRAD has been committed to it from the beginning and they don't seem open to using more research-based materials."

MOVE IT Math actually started as a professional development program for teachers, showing them how to teach mathematical concepts more efficiently. Ann Stiles, a former math teacher in a Project GRAD feeder system who became math manager for Project GRAD–USA, said she and her colleagues knew that the techniques they had tried before hadn't worked. But they also didn't grasp the complexity of translating theories of effective math instruction into a sequence of daily lessons. Stiles later served on a team of Houston teachers who developed the first MOVE IT Math curriculum for Project GRAD. However, she acknowledged that the initial attempt didn't reflect school district requirements, grade-level objectives, extended problem-solving strategies, warm-ups and reviews, or the format of state-mandated tests. Stiles said, "When I look at those first teaching plans, I laugh at how little they took into account the district requirements and how simple we thought this could be."

Project GRAD eventually bought the licensing rights to use MOVE IT Math and adapt the program and training as necessary. In addition to aligning the math lessons with district and state standards and tests, Project GRAD increased and adapted training for the math consultants who work in schools, believing that it is more efficient and effective for the on-campus specialists to coach teachers than to continually bring staffs to a central location for professional development.

All Project GRAD elementary schools receive a math curriculum resource library, which they can supplement with lesson plans compiled on the organization's Web site. Project GRAD currently maintains a computerized database of more than 1,000 suggested math lessons that cover the seven primary curriculum strands, and new teachers receive 20 fully developed lesson plans to help with the first days of school. Teachers can turn to MOVE IT Math-produced props, games, and animated characters to reinforce concepts. For example, solving problems with plastic "fraction cakes" enables children to visualize the relationship of parts to the whole. A game of mathematical "tug-of-war" shows them how to add positive and negative integers. Using basic algorithms, youngsters can learn to subtract numbers with trades.

HISD's Robert Stockwell said district curriculum specialists originally complained that MOVE IT Math did not fully integrate the state's standards and tests. And some of them took umbrage at Project GRAD's "shadow district" of curriculum consultants and coaches. He said most of those conflicts have passed, however, "and I'm hearing good reports about the steps taken to modify and mold math in better alignment."

Resolving the differences has led to a deeper understanding of what steps are necessary to teach urban students well, Stockwell said. He also believes that the level of precision that educators are seeking with the math and reading curricula in Project GRAD schools transcends many other efforts to improve the outcomes for urban students.

"For Project GRAD to work state by state and city by city, I think these kinds of issues have to be surfaced and addressed," Stockwell said. "There is no perfect program across all states."

PART II

SCALING UP

Chapter 7

BALANCING INTIMACY WITH GROWTH

For every Project GRAD scholar who succeeds in college, at least one significant person paved the way. Usually it was a teacher, a counselor, a scholarship coordinator, or an outside mentor, sometimes several people, who let the students know they were capable of excelling and who offered the tools that made their high achievement possible.

These guides steered them to scholarships, drove them to colleges, edited their application essays, counseled them by telephone and e-mail, and in some cases opened their homes to students who didn't have homes of their own. Such personal connection with dedicated adult advocates, people whom they do not wish to disappoint, largely determines whether first-generation students stay in school.

The structural supports that Project GRAD put in place for teachers, students, and families make it possible for impoverished communities to aspire collectively. Extensive professional development, consistent curricula, and a local organization that raises money and distributes resources—these contributions ensure that students in Project GRAD schools will have more than desire behind their climb to college. But such factors are not effective without the personal attention from adults who help them break the cycle of poverty and low expectations.

For Davis High School graduates Felipe Hernandez, Gerardo De Leon, and Octavio "Chavo" Peña, the spark came from Mike Moran, a former Tenneco employee who mentored the three students during high school and college. "I have told friends that except for this guy I would never have gone" to college, Felipe said. "Coming from a family that didn't go to school, I had no one to tell me about university life. I just expected to graduate from high school and get a job in the neighborhood. I had no ambition. Mike told me what I could look forward to and be."

Teachers and counselors helped Davis graduate Ezekiel Moreno by steering him into the most challenging classes. In one of those courses, Ezekiel found an early professional role model in the first male teacher who shared his ethnicity. He described him: "He was short, he was brown, he was Latino, he was from Texas, he expected you to go to college. . . . He talked about how difficult and challenging college had been for him. Working hard made him feel accomplished, even if he only earned a B. It made me want to study more."

Given the low college completion rates for minority students nationwide, the need for mentors to guide them past the routine rough spots seems clear. Colleges focus on diversity during the admissions process, but generally do a better job of recruiting minority students than retaining them.

This is particularly true for Latinos. A study by the Pew Hispanic Center found that two-thirds of Latino youths initially enroll in non-selective, open-enrollment colleges, which have much lower matriculation rates than competitive colleges (Fry, 2004). Just 13% of Latino students who start at a community college complete a bachelor's degree; the figure is only slightly higher for white students (23%).

The Pew study noted that more selective colleges and universities generally provide stronger mentoring and more financial aid. Yet many Latino students are unaware of these advantages. They typically fail to take college admissions exams, they don't start college immediately after high school, they attend college part time, and they live at home—all factors that contribute to lower post-secondary graduation rates (pp. 10–16).

When they reach college, first-generation students must overcome a wide range of emotional and practical obstacles. The personal connections they established while in high school can mean the difference between stopping and staying. In the early years of Project GRAD, many adults willingly filled those critical roles. But the larger the organization grows and the farther it moves from its roots at Davis High School, the more people worry that new leaders won't provide the same degree of support.

Consider the Davis High School graduates who have been accepted at top universities. Ruth Kravetz, the veteran math teacher, has guided almost all of the students without additional compensation. She also keeps track of them through e-mail and telephone once they enter college. In 1997,

Kravetz started the first Advanced Placement calculus class at Davis, teaching the same group of students for 2 years so they could complete both the AB and the BC portions of the course. About 20 students attempted that rigorous math sequence the first time; Kravetz has taught twice that many in other years.

"What gets the strongest kids to the strongest schools and the moderate kids to go to better universities is two years worth of a teacher, somebody on a regular basis saying, 'This is what you have to do to get to college. This is what you have to do to fill out an application,'" Kravetz stressed. "I have to say, 'Pick a dream school, pick three medium schools you think you can get into. Here's your [application] essay back. No, it's not very good. You can't write the same essay that everybody does about their lives. Do it over.'

"All of the kids who went [to college] out of state except one, I know what their college essays looked like and how their applications looked, and in some cases I know the day they decided to mail them in. In some cases, they were at my house on New Year's Eve to get it in with the right postmark."

Kravetz personally steers about 30 students a year through the college application process and prepares most of them to take the College Board's Advanced Placement exams so they can earn college credit for their high school courses. She meets with them during lunch and before and after school, invites them to her home on weekends, consults with their parents, and keeps them focused on the future.

"The schools that are sending lots of kids to good schools [colleges], you can pick one or two teachers who do that cycle of talking with them," Kravetz said. "There has to be some outside force compensating for the family saying, 'We'd rather you stay at home.'"

MENTORS MATTER

Mike Moran was 26 years old and just out of graduate school when Tenneco asked him to mentor some freshmen at Davis High School. He had a brother the same age as the kids and the company agreed to provide a van for mentors to travel to their semimonthly meetings, so Moran signed up.

It was 1991 and the young pipeline analyst didn't know much about Jim Ketelsen's ongoing efforts at Davis. Project GRAD wasn't yet a vision. Moran just wanted to help.

At first, Moran was responsible for eight teenagers at Davis. They talked about education, sports, careers, or whatever else was on their minds. When another mentor moved to a different company, Moran inherited his group as well, finishing the school year with 16 teenagers in tow.

Two years later, just four of those students remained with Moran. By the end of high school, Moran's original group had shrunk to three. Gerardo De Leon, one of those who stayed, said most of the students Moran mentored did graduate from high school but didn't complete college. Gerardo believes that some of the students stopped attending the mentoring sessions because they had other interests, while others couldn't form intimate connections with Moran because of the group's size.

"We didn't know Mike too well when there was a [big] group of us," he said. But Gerardo and his two friends trusted Moran because they knew no one was paying him to come to Davis each week. "He just made us feel that we were somebody. He looked into our lives."

Pairing students with mentors has never been a requirement of Project GRAD, only a desire to provide another helping hand to students who need many steadying influences. But over the years, as students like Gerardo have related the critical influence of mentors, Project GRAD has developed firmer guidelines for schools to improve the training provided to mentors. Even so, both Project GRAD and the mentors recognize that the arrangements depend on successful personality match-ups and adequate time commitments from both the teenagers and the adults.

Research and experience confirm that two of the essential ingredients for effective mentor partnerships are strong connections between the adult and child—a bond that usually forms because of their similar interests—and regular involvement in activities that enable them to have fun together as well as to work on practical goals (Freedman, 1991). Moran said he probably worked so well with Felipe, Gerardo, and Octavio because all of them shared a passion for sports and because he frequently interacted with the boys outside of school.

Nevertheless, Moran had little guidance when he started working at Davis High School. In his initial meetings with the students, he dutifully passed out a few get-acquainted worksheets that the school had provided. Mostly, though, he just talked with the kids, took them on outings, and emphasized the importance of attending college. He also kept showing up.

"I think what encouraged me is that he put a lot of effort and time into us," Octavio Peña said. "That really surprised me, and I thought I owed him something for that. You know, he was trying, and I better try, too."

Studies show that mentor relationships can produce a slew of positive benefits, ranging from better behavior to higher grades in school. The stronger the connection and the longer the partners meet, the greater the potential for success. The opposite can also be true, however. Mentor relationships that end abruptly may cause a neglected child to feel abandoned and more worthless than before.

Moran actually increased his commitment as Gerardo, Felipe, and Octavio advanced through high school. He showed up at their athletic events, took them to see professional sports teams in the area, and drove them to Texas A&M University, his alma mater, located about 90 miles from Houston. On holidays from school, the boys would ride the bus downtown to visit Moran at work and eat lunch with him in the company cafeteria. When it was time to apply to colleges, Moran recruited business associates to write letters of recommendation for the three boys, paid their application fees, and took them to his downtown office to prepare their essays and resumes.

He encouraged all three boys to apply to Texas A&M and apply to Southwest Texas State University in San Marcos, Texas, and Blinn Junior College in Brenham, Texas as backups. He was disappointed when Texas A&M didn't take a chance on the three boys because he believes that the state's public university system has an obligation to reach out to motivated students from poor families.

"A school like A&M, sixty years ago it took farm boys off tractors and put them in college, and then they went back to those towns and built roads and businesses," Moran said. "Now the demographics are different. People don't live in rural areas as much, but the politics have hurt the kids" who replaced them. When they apply to college, "they get up against kids like my brother who've had advanced calculus and amazing SAT scores and yet have none of the common sense and drive and extras that kids like Gerardo, and Octavio, and Felipe have."

Gerardo needed all of those extras to overcome his performance on the college entrance exam and a history of weak instruction in school. His highest combined score on the SAT was 650, despite the fact that he had taken the exam three times. An only child, he said his parents encouraged him to go to college, but both had emigrated from Mexico and didn't know how to pay for or prepare him for higher education.

Gerardo attended bilingual classes in elementary school, which caused him to be placed in a low academic track at Marshall Middle School. When the boys he was associating with drifted into gangs, Gerardo's parents intervened and made him find other friends. Every one of the boys in the original group eventually committed felonies in high school and ended up in prison, Gerardo said.

At Davis, Gerardo's mother fought to get him into more challenging courses, at one point ignoring the advice of the staff and signing a paper saying she wouldn't hold the school responsible if he didn't succeed. A few educators pushed him to excel, Gerardo said, but many signaled their low expectations.

"Teachers really looked down on us, that we weren't going to make it," Gerardo recalled. "They don't tell you directly, but indirectly they let you know that you're not good enough."

Researchers have found that when students get tracked into low-level courses, teachers tend to have low opinions of the students' ability to think deeply about topics and engage in creative exercises. They often believe they are doing the children a favor by not challenging them. In schools serving a high percentage of poor and minority populations, low expectations soon permeate the entire culture until even the brightest, most motivated students have a hard time reaching state and national academic standards (Pathways to College Network, 2002).

Poor and minority families rarely receive good advice about academic programs and do not understand the magnitude of the decisions they make about course selection in middle and high school (LeTendre, 2000). Because schools tend to offer different curricula depending on program designations, students from poor and minority families often discover too late that they lack the proper credentials for college.

When Texas A&M rejected him, Gerardo headed to Blinn Junior College. At Blinn, he found a faculty accustomed to helping students with academic deficiencies. Yet despite small classes and assistance from professors, he was quickly overwhelmed. He dropped his freshman English class after the first week because he didn't know how to write the essays required for the course. Later, he met a girl who taught him how to write college-level papers and he reciprocated by teaching her how to speak Spanish.

After 2 years at Blinn, Gerardo reapplied to A&M and was rejected a second time, although the admissions staff recommended that he complete three additional courses at Blinn and try again. During his third year at the junior college, he became a school cheerleader and received a scholarship that paid for his tuition, fees, and books. Communities in Schools also helped him find a part-time job tutoring and coaching delinquent children.

Throughout college, Gerardo kept in touch with Moran. By this time, his mentor had married and his wife had given birth to triplets. When he had time off from school, Gerardo visited Moran and his family at their home in Tomball, Texas.

After 3 years at Blinn, Gerardo earned one of the last slots in Texas A&M's College of Education. He had planned to pursue a business degree like his mentor, but realized that with a C-plus average in junior college and shaky math skills, he didn't have much chance of succeeding. As happy as he was finally to have a place at A&M, Gerardo found the experience more difficult than he had imagined.

"I didn't tell my parents, but I cried for a whole week, thinking, 'How am I going to make it?'" he said. "How can I tell my mentor, my parents that I'm not going to make it?"

Gerardo didn't have enough money to pay for school, his grades declined, and he resented his relentless hardships, believing that if his parents were richer, if his high school had been better—on and on through all kinds of scenarios—he wouldn't have had to struggle so much in college. In a testament to his character, however, he pushed past the bitterness, telling himself: "You just got to earn it."

In 2001, after 6½ years, he completed college and earned a teaching certificate. Moran bought him an A&M class ring. Today, Gerardo De Leon teaches physical education and coaches at Ketelsen Elementary School in Houston, down the street from his old middle and high schools.

His buddies did well, too. Felipe Hernandez earned a bachelor's degree in Geographic Information Systems in 2000 after 5½ years at Southwest Texas State University. He now manages databases for Conneco, a major oil and gas producer.

Octavio Peña dropped out of Southwest Texas State to care for his ailing mother then spent a year at Houston Community College before accepting a full-time job at a local credit union, where he has received several promotions. He plans to return to college and complete an associate's degree. He is married, raising two children—one of them a stepchild—and trying to buy his first house.

Gerardo has had the most regular contact with Moran, but all three members of the original mentoring group stay in touch by telephone or e-mail.

"He was pretty much our main spark," Gerardo said. "I mean, he was there for us."

BIGGER, NOT NECESSARILY BETTER

After hearing about the hardships that Project GRAD scholars such as Gerardo faced in college, leaders of the Houston organization decided to extend their support network for students beyond high school. Beginning with the Davis, Yates, and Wheatley graduating classes of 2002, they paired the Project GRAD scholars with business volunteers who agreed to mentor them during college. Unable to find a mentor for every student, they focused first on the graduates who were attending colleges outside Houston.

When the students returned to Houston during the winter holidays, however, Project GRAD discovered that many had not been in contact with their mentors during the first semester. Two major problems emerged. First, the students had limited contact with the mentors before they left for college and, thus, hadn't established relationships that were strong enough to overcome the awkwardness of asking a stranger for help long distance. Second, many of the students didn't have their own computers, which made it difficult to communicate regularly by e-mail as planned.

Shanya Gensior, who was director of scholarships for Project GRAD–Houston, said she learned to give students more time to get to know their mentors before they leave for college, and to give the mentors the students' school and home telephone numbers in addition to their e-mail addresses.

Project GRAD organizations in other cities are interested in Houston's experience with mentors and plan to set up their own high school-to-college transition programs to keep their scholars on track to graduate. In Los Angeles, for example, where 182 students from San Fernando High School earned Project GRAD scholarships in 2003, the local Project GRAD organization paid the expenses for one top student to visit Yale and Stanford so she could make an informed decision about which college to attend. Although she had been leaning toward Stanford because it was close to home, the student chose Yale based on the campus visit. Before all the San Fernando students left for college, staff members at Project GRAD–Los Angeles organized a formal send-off party where they distributed school and dorm room supplies. Then they followed up by sending care packages with homemade cookies and handwritten notes to all the students enrolled in colleges outside Los Angeles. Staff members also gave their cell phone numbers to students they had worked with during high school.

Such interventions can help first-generation college students maintain their resolve when academic and emotional challenges cause them to struggle. But nurturing intimate relationships with hundreds of students can tax even the most organized staff. Project GRAD–Los Angeles plans to hire a college liaison to work directly with the graduates. The organization also intends to develop an online database that includes a detailed profile of all the graduates, tracks their grades and experiences in college, and identifies the high school courses that helped or hindered them. Eventually, Project GRAD–Los Angeles intends to collect and computerize academic profiles of all 20,000 students enrolled in the Project GRAD schools in order to spot achievement trends and problems.

As the stories of the Project GRAD scholars demonstrate, one of the key challenges for Project GRAD in its second decade will be balancing intimacy with growth. That is, the organization must find a way to encourage strong, personal bonds between students and adult advocates while expanding the reform program so thousands of other deserving youths receive the same opportunities to excel.

Gensior recalled the collaboration that made student success possible at Davis: The principal who set the standard; the counselors who arranged class schedules so students could meet the scholarship requirements; the teachers who raised their expectations and improved their instruction; the summer institute coordinators who encouraged students to attend the programs; the business and community leaders who raised money and opened doors; and the students who worked harder than they ever had before.

"When I remember the evolution of it, when I remember the change in the faculty, when I remember how everybody talked scholarship, how teachers would invite me to their classrooms and say, 'When are you going to talk to my kids about college scholarships,' I don't see that on every [Project GRAD] campus," Gensior said. "It's way too important for more people not to give it more priority. Not just Project GRAD, but going to college. The person on the front line, it needs to be their passion, not their job."

History has stacked huge odds against minority students succeeding in college. Only 16% of Latino high school graduates and 21% of African-American high school graduates earn a 4-year university degree by age 29, compared with 37% of white high school graduates (Navarro, 2003). Yet there is little variation in the initial hopes of the different student populations. About 80% of African-American and Latino 8th graders say they plan to attend college, compared with 88% of students overall in this age group (Venezia, Kirst, & Antonio, n.d.). This suggests that high school is where the dream gets deferred.

By the end of the 10th year of awarding scholarships in the Davis High School feeder pattern, 1,108 graduates had entered college with assistance from Project GRAD. As inspiring as that number is, the struggle to raise the college completion rate continues at Davis and other Project GRAD high schools.

One ongoing impediment is money. Most students who complete college do so at considerable personal expense because government and university grants have failed to keep pace with tuition increases. For example, from 1992 to 2001, tuition at 4-year public colleges and universities rose faster than family income in 41 states (National Center for Public Policy and Higher Education, 2000).

In 1986 the average federal Pell Grant, available to the neediest students, covered 98% of tuition costs at public 4-year colleges and universities, but only 57% of those costs on average by 1999. College graduates today accumulate an average educational debt of $27,000, 3½ times the amount carried by students a decade before (Winter, 2003). Whereas need-based grants—which do not have to be repaid—once provided the bulk of assistance, about 70% of college students currently take out loans to pay their way, up from 46% of students who did so in 1990.

Although students at all income levels are borrowing more money for college, students from poor families lead the pack. By 2000, the debt load to attend a 4-year college or university consumed about 25% of a poor family's income, double the rate from 20 years before (National Center for Public Policy and Higher Education, 2000).

Another impediment to college completion is academic preparation. Students from poor families are 3½ times more likely than students from affluent families to be marginally unqualified for 4-year colleges (Venezia, Kirst, & Antonio, n.d.). High school standards are extremely inconsistent, and students who do not attend elite high schools often have little understanding of the skills, courses, and tests they will need to gain admission to college—or how to succeed once they get there. Gerardo De Leon incurred $20,000 in debt during college, in part because he spent so much time in remedial courses, which did not count toward his degree.

"While student finances are very important, the intensity and quality of the secondary school curriculum is the best predictor of whether a student will go on to complete a bachelor's degree," Venezia, Kirst, and Antonio (n.d.) write in *Betraying the College Dream: How Disconnected K–12 and Postsecondary Education Systems Undermine Student Aspirations* (p. 9).

Project GRAD has helped to strengthen courses at the high schools it serves by insisting that participating students complete a college-preparatory program. But because Project GRAD initially focused its curricular changes on the elementary and middle grades and only recently expanded those supports to high schools, some students who earned scholarships discovered too late that they weren't ready for college.

To put their experiences in context, consider that only 32% of all U.S. public high school graduates are believed to have the minimum academic qualifications needed to attend 4-year colleges (Greene & Forster, 2003). The numbers for black and Hispanic students are even lower—just 20% of black and 16% Hispanic students nationwide leave high school "college ready."

Claudia Aguirre can relate to these statistics. A Honduran immigrant and a 2001 graduate of Davis High School, she struggled mightily during her first year at the University of Houston. She recalled attending a college history class, sitting in the first row on the first day. After listening to the professor lecture and thinking it odd that he never stopped to mention what was important to remember for the test, Claudia looked around at the 400 other students in the class and noticed they were busy scribbling in their notebooks. When she later asked her roommate what they were doing, the girl thought Claudia was joking that she didn't know how to take notes during class without prompting from the teacher.

"I think that first year in college, there's only one word to describe it—overwhelming," Claudia said. "It was a completely different experience from what I would ever imagine."

At first, she sought comfort by meeting almost daily with a half dozen Davis graduates who entered the university the same year she did. The new college students commiserated about their difficult courses, the stress of balancing school and part-time jobs, and their inability to find anyone at home who could understand what they were going through. At one point, Claudia, who said she graduated in the top 20% of her class, taught the salutatorian of her high school class how to write a college paper. Everyone seemed to struggle, she said.

"I think that teachers in high school, instead of teaching what they probably learned in college, I think they need to talk about the personal experiences you will encounter in the first semester. Not just the work, but how stressed and tense and bitter I was every day," Claudia said. "How about saying some of these professors don't care? They would hand me the work and say, 'Okay, see you next week.' You don't have any support whatsoever. That's what they need to tell us."

For several years, scholarship coordinators at Project GRAD high schools have asked college students on semester break to share their experiences with teenagers who need the kind of frank talk Claudia suggests. Coordinators say the sessions are usually well attended, but they don't know whether the high school students really heed the messages until they enroll in college themselves.

When he returns to Davis to talk to students, Ezekiel Moreno confirms Claudia's impression about the sink-or-swim attitudes of many college professors. But he also talks about the financial drain of college.

"I was broke all the time," Ezekiel said.

In addition to the Project GRAD scholarship, a grant from a Houston foundation, and some financial aid, Ezekiel paid the $34,000 annual cost to attend Cornell University with an ROTC scholarship that he earned in exchange for agreeing to serve in the army after graduation. Despite receiving a $150 monthly stipend from the military while in college, he found it difficult to cover his expenses, which included $500–600 a semester for books, $600 a year for health insurance that was required by the university, about $1,600 a year for plane tickets to and from home, and additional amounts for outside food, entertainment, and personal items. Ezekiel also had to cover the portion of his tuition—$2,000 a year—that the university expected his parents to pay. He said he received no financial assistance from his parents, one of whom has only a 2nd-grade education from Mexico, and the other who dropped out of school in Texas in the 9th grade.

Ezekiel worked part-time in a video store near campus while taking a full course load and fulfilling his ROTC duties. Flush with the excitement of new experiences and freedoms and with no one to teach him how to manage his money—another problem that can cause first-generation college students to fall off track—he quickly went into debt. Ezekiel acknowledges spending too much money on pizza, movies, billiards, and fraternity parties. By the time he graduated, he had charged the maximum amounts possible on five major credit cards that he had obtained while in college.

"In hindsight, it wasn't hell," Ezekiel said, "but going through it, I thought it was." He borrowed $16,000 in student loans to pay the extra school expenses, including a summer that he spent studying in Bolivia. In 2002 Ezekiel completed a double major in history and Spanish literature at Cornell and received an officer's commission in the army with a rank of second lieutenant. He traveled overseas in 2003 and supervised 33 soldiers and $1.5 million worth of military equipment during America's war with Iraq. He's now stationed at Ft. Polk, Louisiana, working as a construction engineer.

Ezekiel counsels several Davis High School students by e-mail, visits the campus to speak to students and teachers whenever he's in Houston, and mentors the younger siblings of several friends. The need for careful financial planning is one of the key messages he shares.

"My friends who are going off to college for the first time, their parents will say, 'He doesn't have any money to eat out.' I say, 'Leave him alone, he'll be okay. He has books, he has a place to live.' I wish someone had told me that."

Ezekiel also encourages other young people to defy the stereotype that poor kids can't excel in school. He knows how difficult it can be to stay positive in the midst of poverty and low expectations, remembering how youths from his old neighborhood used to call him "white boy" for daring to achieve. On occasion, Ezekiel said, his mother and brother have hurled the same insult at him, preferring to denigrate his college education than admit their feelings of inferiority. "Sometimes I feel like an outcast," he said.

The difficult transition that Ezekiel Moreno and other poor and minority students experience upon entering college is beginning to draw attention from researchers and policymakers around the United States, although much work remains. The ACT and the Council for Great City Schools collaborated on a recent report, "Creating Seamless Educational Transitions for Urban African American and Hispanic Students," to find out why minority youths still lagged behind white youths in attending and completing college, and to decide what schools could do to improve the situation (Noeth & Wimberly, n.d.). Among the recommendations: Encourage school counselors to begin talking about college preparation in the middle grades, steer all students to college-prep courses, and establish formal and informal relationships with students so they will have a team of adult advocates working on their behalf.

In 2003, the University of Oregon's Center for Educational Policy Research released a guidebook and CD-ROM that outline the skills and knowledge students need to excel during the first year of college (Cavanagh, 2003). The guide, called *Standards for Success*, will be distributed to every public high school in the United States. It includes samples of college-level assignments and acceptable work products.

These suggestions are a direct result of learning from the experiences of first-generation college students who have recounted their successes and failures. Their perseverance can clear the way for others, but only if policymakers and reformers heed their advice about how to prepare disadvantaged youths for higher education.

As a Project GRAD scholar from Yates High School in Houston put it, any organization that wants to help first-generation college students succeed should never lose sight of the importance of establishing strong personal connections that don't end at the classroom door.

"Until you understand the community where they come from, you'll never understand the child," the college sophomore said. "You'll never understand what they're going through. All you're doing is sending a battered and abused child to college, and they don't even know how to use" the help.

Chapter 8

LEARNING TO CHANGE

When executives of seven Project GRAD sites convened in New York City in the spring of 2002, the occasion should have given cause for hearty congratulations. A school reform initiative that had sprouted in a single feeder system in Houston in 1994 had subsequently taken root in schools serving more than 100,000 students around the country. Test scores at most of the participating schools were increasing, new cities were clamoring to join the organization, and the federal government and private donors were investing $65 million in practices that had produced a slew of first-generation college students.

But as the 3-day meeting got underway, anxiety, not elation, proved to be the common emotion. While the rapid growth of Project GRAD certainly pleased those who had helped to nurture it, the expansion had created tensions aplenty.

Executives in some of the first cities to join worried that the new members might drain the available money and support. Cities that had adopted all of the Project GRAD components wondered why other communities had received exemptions. One city was in the process of ending its relationship with Project GRAD, and executives of two other local organizations had moved on. All the directors wished they could get targeted help—meaning less interference in some cases and more assistance in others—from Project GRAD–USA, the national organization that had incorporated just 1 year before to provide technical and financial resources to the local groups.

Meanwhile, the directors learned that Steven Zwerling, the Ford Foundation official who had provided critical financial support to Project GRAD, would become the new president and chief executive officer of Project GRAD–USA.

"My own assessment at this point is a C-plus," Zwerling said, referring to Project GRAD–USA. "It seems to me not too bad, but I think we have some work to do."

Project GRAD's successes continually stimulated new interest, but the fast expansion also threatened to become the organization's undoing. Initially, Project GRAD operated as a loosely organized network without defined membership fees or rules. The organization welcomed new cities with few restrictions.

In Newark and Nashville, for example, local philanthropists took charge of bringing Project GRAD to their respective communities. While these supporters consulted with school district and university leaders, the decision to join Project GRAD preceded full involvement of the teachers and principals who would be responsible for making the reforms work. Not surprisingly, the educators' understanding of Project GRAD and their willingness to incorporate all of its recommended practices varied greatly from school to school.

Other unexpected problems included conflicts between the training that Project GRAD provided to teachers and limitations imposed through union contracts, math and reading programs that local or state experts favored over Success for All and MOVE IT Math, and the impact of frequent changes in state-mandated tests on Project GRAD's ability to establish benchmarks for tracking student progress. Project GRAD also didn't specify at the beginning precisely how much money each school district and local support organization must commit to the partnership—and what they could expect in return.

To use a business analogy, the process was akin to offering to franchise a specialty store whose popularity has outgrown the first site. While continually improving the products and service at the initial store, the founders also have to pay attention to the development of new sites: learning the peculiarities of their individual markets; ensuring the standards that made the first store so successful; and helping the newcomers negotiate with suppliers, train employees, and evaluate each store's performance. Because the first store couldn't manage both local and national operations, a coordinating organization forms to keep the new federation together. Over time, however, the arrangement becomes uncomfortable. While the directors of the local franchises appreciate the value of the practices that attracted them to the project, they also want to try some innovations. The question was: How much could they change the various components before people stopped recognizing the brand or trusting its quality?

By not anticipating these challenges, Project GRAD wasted some resources and goodwill that slowed progress in the first group of schools that joined after the Davis feeder system in Houston. But those setbacks, in turn, prompted changes that helped the organization codify some essential features of systemic education reform. As it moved from creating a set of reforms to building the capacity of schools to sustain those changes, Project GRAD also made some discoveries that can inform the field of education policy.

THE CONTEXT FOR REFORM

One of the key lessons is the need to understand the local context for reform. An outside organization must have prior knowledge of the politics at play in a school district and anticipate both the probable reactions and the appropriate responses. Who must be included in key discussions? Who can broker new alliances, and who will try to sabotage them? Will early supporters stick around after the public announcements, or will their departures create hard feelings among those who have to live with the changes they endorsed? Do district curriculum specialists favor different reading, math, and classroom management programs, or will they help champion yours? What previous experience does the school system have with education reform, and will those memories help or haunt you?

"When you work with local sites, there's some basic assumptions that you need to deal with," said Dr. Hector Garza, president of the National Council for Community and Education Partnerships and a senior adviser to the Ford Foundation and Project GRAD president Steven Zwerling. He continued, "We're talking about constant change in school leadership, constant turmoil over finances, constant restructuring . . . Education reform in impoverished communities requires double or triple duty. It requires an army of committed individuals who know the vision and are willing to commit to it in a very highly coordinated way."

There wasn't anything strategic about the first Project GRAD spin-offs. Essentially, the partnerships resulted from Jim Ketelsen's determination to test his reform model in other communities and the school districts' desperation to taste something besides failure. Project GRAD welcomed the first cities with a simple memorandum of understanding that spoke of each partner's commitment to reform.

In 1998 and 1999, when Project GRAD moved into Newark and Los Angeles, respectively, its limited track record as a reform model meant that only school systems under siege took a second look. To its credit, Project GRAD didn't recoil from the frightening visions of urban education that these school districts presented.

In 1995, after a 10-year investigation, state officials had gained control of the 45,000-student Newark school district (Keller, 2000), citing widespread corruption and mismanagement and charging that the system had been "at best flagrantly delinquent and at worst deceptive in discharging its obligations to the children enrolled in the public schools" (*Education Week*, 1998). In the areas targeted by Project GRAD, students' average scores on nationally standardized tests, which had already fallen into the lowest tier, declined steadily the longer they stayed in school (Ham, Doolittle, & Holton, 2000). Only 45% of Newark students graduated from high school, and just half of those students went to college.

In Los Angeles, a sprawling, disjointed system whose 700,000 students attend some of the most overcrowded schools in the nation, three different superintendents had moved in and out of office in the 4 years prior to Project GRAD's arrival. Students attended school on alternating year-round tracks to relieve building congestion, but the schedules meant that some children couldn't get the courses they needed to graduate on time and that some teachers couldn't participate in training designed to improve their instruction. The latter problem was particularly vexing because 60% of the 4,500 new teachers hired in Los Angeles during the 1996–97 school year held emergency credentials (*Education Week*, 1998). A study conducted in 2001 and 2002 by the Evaluation and Training Institute for Project GRAD–Los Angeles (2002) found that only 2% of the teachers in the San Fernando High School feeder system believed that all of their students "would be prepared to do college preparatory coursework in the future" and just 19% believed that all their students "were capable of grade-level performance."

"Project GRAD is still a bottom feeder," Zwerling said of the organization's work with the most troubled school systems in America. "It's not the world in the middle."

Given those constraints, achieving progress would be difficult for any comprehensive reform initiative, much less one like Project GRAD, which works with small groups of schools operating within much larger school systems. Yet the limited control that an outside organization can exert on the school district bureaucracy is precisely why reformers must understand the local context for change.

For example, Newark presented many different issues than Houston, and Project GRAD stumbled as it tried to replicate the model that had been successful in Texas. State interference was a constant source of tension. A 1998 New Jersey Supreme Court ruling had restricted Newark and 29 other poor districts to using "proven, effective" whole-school designs. Success for All, one of Project GRAD's components, was the state's preferred reform model for elementary schools, but Project GRAD wasn't specifically mentioned. The organization's backers eventually obtained an exemption so schools could adopt Project GRAD in conjunction with other reform models. However, the multiplicity of programs caused Project GRAD to be treated as an add-on feature in many schools instead of being the focus for everything that happens in the building.

Eight other reform models coexist in the schools that Project GRAD supports in Newark. Malcolm X. Shabazz and Central high schools, for example, are part of the Talent Development network at Johns Hopkins University, which emphasizes career academies and separate 9th-grade houses to create small learning communities within larger schools. Although high school administrators believe that Talent Development and Project GRAD are complementary—both programs emphasize building relationships with students and guiding them to college—they call Project GRAD their "scholarship program" and Talent Development their "school-wide reform."

Project GRAD's impact in Newark was compromised in other ways. Because of fiscal constraints, the reform initiative operates in just half of the 16-school Shabazz High School feeder system and in only one third of the 18 schools in the Central High School feeder system.[1] So, in addition to coping with a 40% average mobility rate in their schools, educators at

Project GRAD schools continually receive students from nearby schools who have little or no experience with the various components.

Newark's math curriculum differs, too. School district administrators believed the district's curriculum was superior to MOVE IT Math and more closely aligned with the state's content standards. Project GRAD let the Newark schools keep their math program, a decision that caused problems when other cities expected to get similar consideration for their requested exemptions.

Project GRAD announced its partnership with Newark in February 1998 with great fanfare but insufficient preparation. Project GRAD–USA had not formed yet, so there was no lead group to counsel the new participants. Organizers in Houston told Newark school officials that their primary expense would be hiring scholarship coordinators for the high schools, and that outside funders would pick up most of the program costs. Both the state and the local school district ultimately incurred substantial costs to support Project GRAD in Newark. (In 2003, the Newark Public Schools contributed 60% of Project GRAD's costs.)

At the start, Lucent Technologies provided the main financial support for Project GRAD in Newark, which is located about 18 miles from Lucent's headquarters. Several Lucent executives took positions with Project GRAD–Newark and its board of directors. By 2002, the Lucent Foundation had donated more than $11 million to Project GRAD's operations in the city's schools. Only the Ford Foundation's contributions of $7.8 million came close to that amount.

The problem was that Lucent became so identified with Project GRAD–Newark that other area foundations were slow to donate. Project GRAD's backers also did not cultivate broad community connections from the beginning. For instance, the Newark-based Victoria Foundation has donated only $50,000 to Project GRAD, a fraction of the $1 million the foundation contributed to the Newark public schools in 2002 and the $5 million it contributed in 1996 to support local reforms stemming from the state's takeover of the district.

"Fundraising, to be truthful, it's been quite challenging," said Dr. Rudolph Frank, a Lucent vice president who chairs the Project GRAD–Newark board.

Adopting the Project GRAD reform model proved difficult as well. Leaders from the school district, the business community, and the local teachers' union traveled to Houston to observe the Texas schools in action, and staff members from Project GRAD–Houston traveled to Newark to lend assistance, but there was no formal method identified for transplanting the various components. Newark was just supposed to copy what Houston had done.

Zwerling said he and others didn't initially grasp the complexities involved in moving a reform model to another city. Newark and other early partners needed more support than the fledgling Project GRAD organization could provide. "This is really [about] adaptation, not replication," he continued. "If I had done it again, I would have encouraged the development of Project GRAD–USA right away. That was a major mistake."

Teachers at Shabazz High School learned about Project GRAD the day the partnership was announced at their campus. Mary Bennett, the school's principal who later became executive director of Project GRAD–Newark, said the sponsors prohibited her from telling her staff about the partnership in advance. Instead, she spent several months after the public announcement meeting with small groups of teachers, students, and parents to explain Project GRAD and encourage their participation.

"I think that to a very large extent folks felt obliged to adopt this reform because, one, it was coming from the superintendent and, two, it wasn't costing anything during the startup," Bennett said. "So, even though there was a lot of expressed reservations about it, folks felt they had to do it."

Because the Newark Teachers Union had what President Joseph Del Grosso termed an "adversarial relationship" with the state-appointed superintendent, Dr. Beverly Hall, who later moved to Atlanta, Project GRAD also didn't get off to a strong start in some schools. For example, when Project GRAD tried to hire college students and some noncertified teachers to provide extra tutoring to students in reading—as the organization had done in Houston—union leaders in Newark balked at what they considered an attempt to circumvent contract restrictions against privatizing work that belonged to school district employees. Union leaders said they wanted to ensure that students learned from certified teachers.

Project GRAD eventually worked with the school district to hire reading tutors according to the union's terms, but the arrangement proved more expensive and less effective than anticipated. School leaders said they had to accept the most senior applicants, who were not necessarily the most qualified reading instructors. Del Grosso attributed any problems to "personality conflicts" that the union would agree to look at "on a case-by-case basis."

The missteps that Project GRAD took in the beginning of its relationship with the Newark schools led to inconsistent implementation of the reform components. At the elementary level, Project GRAD has spurred significant achievement gains. The percentage of 4th graders passing the state's reading proficiency exam nearly tripled in the Central feeder system from 2000 to 2002, and rose 3½ times in the Shabazz feeder system during the same period, compared to doubling for the district as a whole (New Jersey Department of Education, 2002). Elementary teachers and principals generally use and appreciate Success for All, Consistency Management, and Communities in Schools.

"I love this program," Belinda Bush, a teacher at Dayton Street School, said about Success for All. During the 90-minute daily reading block, Bush works with 16 3rd through 5th graders, including one special-education student, all of whom have progressed to a 6th-grade reading level. "It pushes them more. They all want to strive."

In Dayton's technology lab, science teacher Arthur Franklin and the staff of Communities in Schools set up a Junior Science Wizard program where they show students how to use lab equipment, design science experiments, and make community presentations. In the fall of 2002, 6th, 7th, and 8th graders worked together on a proposal that they planned to take to city government requesting that a community center and shopping mall be part of a neighborhood revitalization plan.

Franklin, who joined Dayton Avenue's staff after nearly 25 years in other school districts, said it was easy to incorporate Project GRAD's components into his teaching repertoire. The classroom managers and warm-up activities recommended by Consistency Management have been especially effective with students: "It brings out the leadership skills" of the children, Franklin said.

Meanwhile, Shabazz High School has made sporadic progress after 5 years with Project GRAD. Just 30 graduates met the requirements for the Project GRAD scholarship in 2001, 26 did so in 2002, and 25 met the mark in 2003. At the beginning of the 2002–03 school year, only 18% of the freshmen at Shabazz had signed covenants agreeing to abide by the terms of the Project GRAD scholarship, compared to 89% of the freshmen at Central High School. By the end of the school year, the vice principal in charge of the Freshman Academy at Shabazz had worked with Project GRAD–Newark to increase the scholarship commitments to 65% of the freshman class, but many Shabazz families seem to be skeptical or disinterested in the college scholarship offer.

District administrators and Project GRAD managers attribute the low numbers at Shabazz to inconsistent support from the school staff. Until 2001, for example, Shabazz manually calculated students' grade-point averages and didn't measure every child's progress. Consequently, some students discovered too late that their academic records wouldn't qualify them for a Project GRAD scholarship. Of the 50 potential Project GRAD scholars identified at the start of the 2002–03 school year, only 26 still had a 2.5 grade-point average after the first semester.

Discipline problems also impede progress at Shabazz. About 10% of the students arrive late most days, according to teachers, and after they receive tardy slips, many of the latecomers roam the halls and distract students already in class. A sign on the office bulletin board in the fall of 2002 congratulated the 29 Shabazz teachers who had earned a score of 80 or better during a recent Consistency Management observation. But there are about 100 faculty members at Shabazz, which means that nearly two-thirds couldn't provide evidence that they were actively using the recommended techniques for classroom management.

In response to these problems, the Ford Foundation agreed to pay for a curriculum specialist to work with the two high school faculties, and Bennett has been meeting regularly with the administrators to resolve training and implementation issues. The scholarship coordinator at Shabazz keeps track of upperclassmen who have at least a 2.3 grade-point average, and requires daily progress reports, signed by their teachers, so she knows whether they attended class. Project GRAD–Newark expanded its SAT prep program, started an after-school tutoring session, and created a Saturday morning tutoring session, modeled after Project GRAD–Atlanta's Zapping Zeroes program, where struggling juniors and seniors can receive extra help to raise their grades. In addition, the principal at Shabazz asked each department chairperson to mentor 15 to 20 seniors through the school year so fewer of them will fall off the path to college.

To correct some of the organizational problems encountered in Newark and other early sites, Project GRAD now signs detailed contracts with participating communities—one with the local organizations that coordinate the reforms, and one with the school districts. Project GRAD also spends time with union representatives, curriculum specialists, and school board members in each community to address their concerns and seek their approval.

"In the past, we didn't require school district approval. We kind of let the local organization and district decide how to" gain support, but that process often created turmoil, said Stephanie Smith-Arce, director of implementation and site expansion for Project GRAD–USA. She added, "In some communities, like Columbus, because the [teachers'] union was not brought fully aboard at the start of the initiative, there have been continuous" problems gaining teachers' support for the programs.

In another example, she noted, Project GRAD–Cincinnati began without a public endorsement of support from the full school board. This oversight caused problems when a new superintendent took over in Cincinnati and Project GRAD didn't have the leadership backing to ensure that the school reforms would proceed as designed. "We have to involve both the district and the community side," Smith-Arce said. "I think that's what hasn't been done" in every case.

The Project GRAD experience in Akron, Ohio demonstrates the difference that the new emphasis on coalition building can mean to a community. Before Akron adopted Project GRAD in 2002, national organizers spent time addressing the concerns of local school board members, central office administrators, principals, teachers, parents, and business and civic representatives. In turn, the community quickly rallied in support of the recommended changes and developed new methods of promoting them. For example, principals of the six participating schools in Akron decided to bag groceries at a neighborhood supermarket one Saturday so they could explain Project GRAD to parents as they moved through the checkout lines.

Akron was also among the first cities to use Project GRAD's 81-page *New Site Handbook* and a refined Memorandum of Understanding that

Project GRAD asks each affiliate organization to sign. The latter identifies five distinct phases—exploratory, development, approval, implementation, and postimplementation—and the steps that each party must take to ensure success. The 10 requirements of the exploratory phase include involving educators and community representatives in the decision-making process and assembling a diverse group to serve on the local organization's board of directors. From Project GRAD's end, the contract language specifying the organization's duties suggests a greater effort to collaborate. The word "monitor" appears only once on the list; every other responsibility is denoted by the words "develop," "support," and "provide."

"That's a significant difference because we used to say 'do the program' and not be mindful of what was [already] in place," said Robert Rivera, the former TMO community organizer in Houston, who later became executive director of Project GRAD–USA. "There are some things that the schools are doing well that should continue, and we should support that, or standards that the state sets up for the school districts in terms of achievement levels. We have to be respectful of those and try to help the school districts achieve their goals. It's understanding the school district's interests much more than we did before."

STRONG NON-PROFIT ORGANIZATIONS

Another key lesson from Project GRAD's expansion is the need to develop strong non-profit organizations to coordinate education reforms in each community. In the same way that local education funds act as "conveners and brokers" (Brophy, 2001) to unite people with different interests, non-profit organizations affiliated with Project GRAD help educators work with other community members to improve the public's schools.

The composition and responsibilities of the local coordinating organization were not clearly defined at the beginning of Project GRAD. For example, Nashville didn't set up an independent organization: faculty members at Vanderbilt University coordinated the work. The unconventional arrangement came about as a result of venture capitalist W. Mc-Comb "Mac" Dunwoody's desire to help Project GRAD expand. At the suggestion of his daughter, Katharine, who had graduated from Vanderbilt and wanted to assist the local public schools, Dunwoody decided to bring Project GRAD to Nashville. The Project GRAD proposal subsequently ended up in the office of the assistant provost, Marcy Singer-Gabella, who became the first executive director of Project GRAD–Nashville in 1999.

Vanderbilt had collaborated with the public schools on many occasions, and faculty members in the university's education department had promoted partnerships stemming from their research into various instructional practices. While Singer-Gabella and her colleagues believed in the value of Project GRAD's structural components and scholarship support for students, they were less enamored with the curricular features. Some Nashville schools had had previous negative experiences with Success for All and wouldn't adopt the reading program, Singer-Gabella said, while Vanderbilt had developed a math approach that educators preferred to MOVE IT Math. She said, "When we began suggesting different ways of getting to a shared end, we couldn't come to agreement with Project GRAD."

The philosophical differences were further complicated by internal changes within the Nashville school district. Attendance boundaries for schools in the Project GRAD feeder system were reconfigured three times in 3 years because of the district's desegregation plan. This process reduced the number of schools aligned with Project GRAD from seven to five. In addition, a new superintendent arrived in Nashville and promptly announced his intention to discontinue outside educational partnerships so the schools could focus on fundamentals. The new chief also fired or moved many principals and central office administrators, severing some important personal connections to Project GRAD–Nashville, and he reduced the district's financial contributions to the Project GRAD schools.

"When all of the changes happened, there was no group to step in and advocate," said Zwerling, who acknowledged Project GRAD's failure to require Nashville to form an independent non-profit group at the start.

In July 2002, after months of difficult negotiations, Project GRAD and Nashville officially separated. The Nashville group changed its name to Imagine College. Singer-Gabella, who stayed on as executive director, said the new organization planned to honor the original scholarship agreements as well as to offer college institutes, instructional support for teachers, and social services assistance to families, although not necessarily in the same way that Project GRAD does. In 2003 the first Imagine College graduating class included 50 Nashville students who earned scholarships, 46 of whom subsequently enrolled in college.

Project GRAD's experience in Nashville, where local parties had conflicts with the national organization, is not unusual in the realm of non-profit expansions. To a certain degree, a tug-of-war over ideals and implementation is part of the normal pattern of finding out whether a particular model is a good fit for a local group.

"If replication is to occur and proven ideas are to spread, strong organizations are required both at the local level and at the center," noted Jeffrey Bradach (2003), a business and non-profit analyst who has written about the internal and external pressures on groups as they try to scale up their designs. He continued, "Nevertheless, tension between local sites and the center is almost inevitable, because the particularities of local conditions are rarely 100 percent aligned with the national model. Sooner or later, these discrepancies will create some conflict in the system. The key question is whether the conflict is constructive—producing learning—or destructive."

As a result of its experience in Nashville, Project GRAD now insists that all communities create local non-profit groups to coordinate fund-raising, monitor services, and run interference between the school districts and the national organization. Project GRAD–USA's *New Site Handbook* explains the responsibilities of the governing board and staff members, lists specific suggestions for recruiting a broadly representative group of advocates, and describes the leadership training necessary to build an effective organization. The planning and negotiations must precede Project GRAD's program implementation by at least a year.

The difference between the earlier and later approaches is apparent in Knoxville, where interest in Project GRAD started at the school level and spread to the larger community. Business leaders in Knoxville had learned from previous experience that educators resist school improvement plans that don't involve them from the beginning. An effort in the mid-1990s to turn over the city's lowest-performing elementary school to Edison Schools Inc., the private education management company started by Knoxville native Chris Whittle, had alienated the superintendent, school board members, and educators. After a few years, relations between school and community leaders had improved, thanks to a new, reform-minded superintendent and a local program that persuaded 75 business executives to spend a day observing public school principals on the job. Those visits inspired the principals of three inner-city schools and the three business leaders who shadowed them to form a study group dedicated to finding solutions to the schools' chronically low achievement.

Mike Reynolds, principal of Fulton High School, explained: "I had kind of sketched an idea for an urban [reform] program. As we talked, we filled in the framework for what it would look like: A social work piece, a reading component, a math component, something to unify K–12, and something postsecondary, a discipline piece."

A short time later, while attending an education conference in San Antonio, Reynolds heard about a program that seemed to address each of those needs. Based on his recommendation, school and community leaders traveled to Houston in November 2000 to see Project GRAD in action. The Knoxville-based Cornerstone Foundation paid their way.

"I'll be honest, I was skeptical," said Reynolds. "You've seen so many canned programs that have come down the line. Sometimes, people try to pass off things as being very successful and when you start looking at them, they're not."

Reynolds said he made a point of visiting classrooms that were not on Project GRAD's official tour and talked to teachers and students who confirmed "that this program and the components were having an impact. They were excited about it. It was making a difference."

On the ride back to Knoxville, as members of the tour group discussed all the reasons why Project GRAD wouldn't work in their community, the focus of the conversation suddenly shifted from problems to possibilities. Representatives from the University of Tennessee and Pellissippi State Community College offered to pay for some scholarships and the summer institutes. The president of the Cornerstone Foundation said he would lead a community fund-raising drive. School leaders pledged to get their colleagues on board. Within several months, the small planning group had grown to 80 people, including parents, school board members, and directors of community centers and after-school programs.

In May 2001, a 48-person group from Knoxville traveled to Houston to observe Project GRAD schools for the second time. By this point, the Knoxville group had lined up most of the local financing for Project GRAD, hired an executive director, aligned schools into two feeder systems serving 7,289 students, and gained unanimous support from principals and school board members. Knoxville officially joined Project GRAD beginning with the 2001–02 school year.

"I think if it had been a top-down approach from either side, it wouldn't have happened," said Laurens Tullock, president of the Cornerstone Foundation and a member of the Project GRAD Knoxville board. "I think it has an awful lot to do with not one person being excited but seeing how so many people got excited." Learning how to collaborate, he said, "was as important as finding Project GRAD."

The Knoxville organization eventually formed a 36-member board whose directors are intimately involved in the schools and represent a broad sector of the community. Their enthusiasm for the changes Project GRAD recommended prompted quick progress in the 14 participating schools even before most had implemented all of the components.

Consider some of the preliminary data collected by Project GRAD–Knoxville and the Knox County Public Schools: At tiny Maynard Elementary School, the lowest performing in the city and the first in Knoxville to implement Success for All, the number of students reading at or above grade level rose from 16 to 52 out of the total population of 118 students within the first 9 months. Every Project GRAD school that has implemented Consistency Management reported significant reductions in the number of discipline referrals, including Christenberry Elementary, where the figure dropped by two thirds, and Belle Morris Elementary, where it plummeted from 700 incidents to 200. The 2003 summer college institutes attracted 342 freshmen and sophomores who earned $49,640 in stipends. Austin-East High School's 19% gain on the state's writing exam was greater than that of all other Knox County high schools. Fulton High School surpassed the district average pass rate on the math proficiency exam, and students checked out four times as many books from the school library as they had 2 years before. Campus Family Support teams in the 14 Project GRAD schools handled 3,512 referrals, provided emergency assistance to 407 families, formed 30 student clubs on campus, and conducted 79 academic events that brought 2,774 parents and guardians into the schools during the 2002–03 term.

Project GRAD–Knoxville attributes much of the early success to Superintendent Charles Lindsey's leadership retreats and his personal visits to each of the 14 Project GRAD schools in the spring of 2003. During the campus meetings, the three principals who were instrumental in bringing Project GRAD to Knoxville described their commitment to the reform model. High school students discussed the importance of the college scholarships. Lindsey told the educators that he would honor any transfer requests but expected full compliance from all who chose to stay. Only five teachers asked to leave, he said.

Project GRAD "has as much chance to change the city as anything we have going," said Bill Haslam, past president of Pilot Corp., the new mayor of Knoxville, and chairman of the board of Project GRAD–Knoxville. "It's costly, it's time consuming, it's complicated but I'm convinced it's worth it."

A LOCAL CHAMPION

The third major lesson of Project GRAD's national expansion is the need to recruit a "local champion" whose credibility, commitment, and financial resources will rally others to the cause and help schools sustain change. Atlanta was the city that first showed Project GRAD how sound strategies for involving corporate executives, philanthropists, and educators can improve the reform model's integration into the community's schools. When Dr. Beverly Hall took charge of the Atlanta Public Schools in 1999, she immediately let business and civic leaders know that she wanted to import Project GRAD to assist the lowest-performing schools and, eventually, to shepherd reforms in all local schools. She promised to establish meaningful partnerships between the school system and the larger community.

Business leaders appreciated the message but remained skeptical because they were "very weary of lots and lots of effort [with the public schools] with no results," said Dr. George Brumley,[2] the retired head of pediatrics at Emory University's School of Medicine who became chairman of Project GRAD–Atlanta. "Second, there were a lot of well-intentioned people in multiple places, but they didn't work together."

The frustration among corporate and foundation donors was not unique to Atlanta. After more than a decade of investing billions of dollars in public school reforms nationwide and trying to instill higher standards and accountability, many private donors have begun scaling back or insisting on stricter terms because of the disappointing results of the 1990s (Jones, 2002).

In Atlanta, to many people's surprise, the school district and the corporate community did establish new ties, and Project GRAD was a key catalyst when it moved into the first Atlanta feeder system during the 2000–01 school year. Kweku Forstall, an attorney who had been vice president at the United Way of Metropolitan Atlanta, became executive director of Project GRAD–Atlanta. Hall made good on her promise to collaborate by inviting Forstall to become a member of her cabinet and by inviting Project GRAD's program director to join another district leadership team. In turn, three of the nine Atlanta school board members serve on Project GRAD–Atlanta's board of directors, along with Hall and one of her deputy superintendents. Among the other Project GRAD board members are two college presidents, several senior executives of local corporations and foundations, and the president of the Atlanta PTSA.

"The level of involvement and cooperation between Project GRAD Atlanta and the Atlanta Public Schools is a uniquely positive feature of the Atlanta story," MDRC (2001) noted in a preliminary evaluation.

To promote and protect Project GRAD's interests, Brumley attended almost every school board meeting from 2000 to 2003 (Sabulis, 2003). Along with Hall and the president of the Atlanta Board of Education, Brumley led the drive to raise $20 million to pay for the first 5 years of Project GRAD, contributing $1.2 million from his family's Zeist Foundation. Project GRAD–Atlanta reached its financial goal in less than 2 years.

"He took the lead," Hall said (Sabulis, 2003). "I really do believe that if it were not for his name, and the integrity [of] people attached to him and his family, we would not have reached the $20 million goal."

Brumley's leadership and fund-raising savvy meant that Forstall could concentrate on providing service to schools instead of spending most of his time chasing corporate sponsorships and partners. "We were able to staff to the level we thought was appropriate to ensure quality implementation," Forstall said. "It was key to our initial success."

Project GRAD–Atlanta has spread to two feeder systems with 29 schools, representing about one third of all the schools in the Atlanta district. Sixty-two percent of the students in the Project GRAD elementary schools now read at or above grade level, compared to 29% before the reforms started during the 2000–01 school year (Project GRAD–Atlanta, 2002).

At Washington High School, a nearly all-black school that had posted among the lowest achievement levels in the city and typically sent only about 15% of its graduates to college, students spoke enthusiastically about the impact of Project GRAD. The first group of Project GRAD scholars won't graduate from Washington until 2004. Yet by 2003 nearly half—47%—of the junior and senior classes had earned a 2.5 grade-point average or higher and had attended at least one summer institute. Ninety percent of Washington High School juniors passed the Georgia High School Graduation Test in writing on the first try in 2003, 91% passed the English exam, and 80% passed the math exam. In 2000–01, the first year of Project GRAD, 163 students graduated from Washington High School. The next year, 211 graduated, and 244 graduated the following year. By 2003, 350 seniors were on track to graduate and 148 of them were still eligible for the Project GRAD scholarships.

Christopher, a football and basketball player who wants to be the first in his family to attend a 4-year college, said he was able to study pre-calculus in the 10th grade because of the math preparatory courses he took during the Project GRAD summer institutes. "We have some of the coolest teachers," he said. "They try to make classes as interesting as possible."

"Class has been going a lot smoother since CMCD," noted a sophomore named Jarrett. "Everyone has a job to do."

"I'm the homework manager," explained Carlos, a junior. CMCD "just makes it more fun and better in the classroom. Project GRAD works, for real."

Chapter 9

REACHING OUT TO RURAL AMERICA

Visitors to Tyonek, Alaska must seek permission from the tribal corporation, which manages the village, before landing on the gravel airstrip near the Cook Inlet shoreline. On a day without excessive headwinds, fog, or snowstorms, a chartered plane takes about 45 minutes to reach Tyonek from one of the small towns located along the southwestern coast of the Kenai Peninsula.

The regularly scheduled, twice weekly flights from Soldotna cost $90 each way—not an excessive amount, but certainly pricey for teachers returning to the mainland on weekends or for school district administrators trying to assist educators in the Alaskan Bush.

Passengers departing the airstrip at Tyonek can make a quick hike to Tebughna Elementary and High School, where 37 Dena'ina Athabascan Indian children attend the 1st through 12th grades. The modern, one-story building has a gymnasium, several multigrade classrooms, and a spacious office, but no potable water because the filtration system supplying the town's 180 residents hasn't worked for several months.

Three certified teachers and a 28-year-old principal instruct the children, almost none of whom reads or computes beyond a 5th-grade level. Only 22% of Tebughna's students met Alaska's proficiency standards for language arts in 2003, and 17% reached the targets in math (Dillon, 2003). Students attend classes sporadically, often missing a week or two at a time.

"Next week, half my school will leave" to go moose hunting, first-year principal Matt Fischer said. "In looking at last year's attendance records, it's common for kids to miss forty days a year."

Because of the isolated location, the high cost of food, and the limited housing options, Tebughna's faculty turns over almost every year. Tribal restrictions prevent outsiders from buying property, making it difficult for educators to establish roots in the community. Rental housing is substandard and scarce. During the 2003–04 school year, a male teacher, his young daughter, and a female colleague had to share a musty, four-room trailer that they rented from the school district for $300 per month. On many weekends, they commuted to homes that their respective spouses maintained in other towns.

High unemployment levels, low expectations, and the lure of drugs and alcohol stunt many children's ambitions, but so does the quality of instruction they have received over the years. Some parents complain that their children suffer because the rapid replacement of teachers requires students to continually adapt to different instructional methods and academic standards. Each teacher who joins the staff seems to change everything around, one parent noted, "and the children get confused. They're never moving ahead. They stay stuck."

Although acknowledging that many Tyonek families do not provide proper guidance or value education, observers say a growing number of families understand that their children must stay in school because traditional subsistence hunting and fishing can no longer sustain the village population. Nevertheless, when officials from Project GRAD and the Kenai Peninsula Borough School District showed up in September 2003 to announce that Tebughna was among seven local schools whose faculties opted to join the national reform network, only four Tyonek parents heard the news. Windy conditions had delayed the chartered plane, and few people remained at school after classes had dismissed for the day.

Tebughna High School included three 9th graders and one 11th grader at the time of the visit, but none of the students who were eligible for the Project GRAD scholarships came with their parents to sign the pledge of participation. Many Tyonek teenagers leave the village to attend regional boarding schools because the community "has done such a poor job" of educating them, Fischer said, "and they know it." In a typical year, nine or ten of the high school students will return to Tebughna, suffering from homesickness and acknowledging that they lack the skills to compete in larger, more rigorous schools.

The legacy of low academic achievement in Tyonek prompted one mother to ask the Project GRAD representatives if the promised college scholarships would cover postsecondary vocational training. Parents repeatedly raised that question during Project GRAD's presentations to other school communities in the Kenai Peninsula: Would the scholarships be available to students who pursued something other than a 4-year bachelor's degree?

Heather Pancratz, executive director of Project GRAD–Kenai Peninsula, replied that the local Project GRAD board would make the decision, but Fischer interjected, saying he would use his influence to insist that the scholarships pay for vocational training. Tycene Edd, new site development coordinator for Project GRAD–USA, tried to steer a middle course. She explained that while local high school graduates might want to learn a trade, such as welding, Project GRAD would encourage them to use the vocational training as a stepping stone to a related college-educated profession, such as engineering or architecture.

Then another mother raised her hand to ask a question that many others have wondered about since Project GRAD arrived in the Kenai Peninsula. "How are you guys going to ensure that our kids will get a quality education in rural Alaska when you're used to being in urban settings?" she asked.

Whether an urban school reform design can work in a state with the lowest population density in the nation is the essential challenge of Project GRAD's partnership with the Kenai Peninsula, which represents the first time the organization has tried to expand to rural America. While low-performing schools in the Kenai Peninsula share many problems common to those in inner-city schools, Alaska's size magnifies every issue. The Kenai Peninsula district operates 40 schools within 25,000 square miles, roughly the size of Connecticut. To travel from the northernmost point of the district to the southern tip requires 4 hours of driving time followed by a half-hour plane ride across Kachemak Bay. Three of the seven Kenai Peninsula schools that have joined Project GRAD are accessible only by plane or boat.

The cost of providing educational services escalates when factoring in the distance between the schools and their sparse populations. Project GRAD will serve just 600 students in the Kenai Peninsula, the equivalent of a single elementary school in most other cities within the national organization's network. Officials estimate that it will require about $3,000 per student per year—six times the typical amount—to put Project GRAD in place in Alaska. Project GRAD–Kenai Peninsula, the local non-profit organization set up to support the schools, will bear primary responsibility for raising the money.

The major reason Project GRAD will cost so much in Alaska is that the regular expenses for staff and programs must be spread among fewer students. All but one of the seven Kenai Peninsula schools that agreed to participate in Project GRAD include kindergarten through the 12th grades, so each school will operate as a feeder system unto itself. Project GRAD will hire a full-time coach to work with each school's faculty, and at every site a teacher who agrees to mentor his or her colleagues will receive a $3,000 annual stipend. Both accommodations reflect the difficulty of expecting coaches or consultants to serve multiple schools in the Kenai Peninsula, as they do in other districts affiliated with Project GRAD.

Cultural distinctions must also be factored into planning. Three of the Kenai Peninsula schools aligned with Project GRAD primarily serve Native Alaskan students, and three other schools include a majority of Old Believers. The latter are members of a persecuted sect of the Russian Orthodox Church whose members sought asylum in the United States more than 30 years ago so they could worship and live as their ancestors did in earlier centuries. Traditionally, the Old Believers had little regard or use for formal education. Girls usually married at age 14 or 15, raised large families, and helped their husbands with commercial fishing or farming. Many parents encouraged their children to quit school at age 16, which represents the end of the state's compulsory education. In the Kenai Peninsula's tiny Razdolna School, which includes 32 children from two extended families of Old Believers, no student has graduated from the school since it opened 17 years ago.

Few adults from these remote communities have the credentials to teach, and the pool of accomplished educators willing to relocate or commute is small. Statewide, Native Alaskans account for only 5% of public school teachers (McDowell Group Inc., 2001). In rural Alaska 80% of the teachers come from other states. Although some Kenai Peninsula schools have developed strong attachments to teachers and principals from outside their communities, many families remain distrustful that educators will act in their children's best interests. At Nanwalek Elementary and High School, which serves Sugpiaq children who identify with the Pacific

Eskimo language family, many parents prevent teachers from assigning homework and keep their children away from school whenever educators try to circumvent the unorthodox arrangement.

"It really is a quandary," said Rick Matiya, coordinator of federal programs and a former bilingual specialist in the Kenai Peninsula Borough School District. Although every Nanwalek parent doesn't support the no-homework practices, he said, "the overall value of education is they talk the talk but don't walk the walk. It's okay not to come to school on time. It's okay not to do homework. Then when kids don't do well, it's somebody else's fault."

Such interactions indicate the low educational expectations that some Native Alaskans have for their children, based on their personal experiences with school and their belief that white teachers often discriminate against Native Alaskan students. Forty-two percent of adult Native Alaskans have attained a high school diploma, a GED certificate, or less (Alaska Natives Commission, 1994). Along with other Native American groups, Native Alaskans have the lowest level of college enrollment and completion rates of any minority group in the United States. As a state, Alaska ranks 48th in the number of high school graduates of all races who enroll in college.

In Native Alaskan villages, such as Nanwalek, Tyonek, and Port Graham, three of the Kenai Peninsula schools affiliated with Project GRAD, families often get by on the $1,500 to $1,800 annual dividend checks that Alaska disperses to each resident from the interest generated by the state's oil revenues. Surrounded by large extended families and accustomed to living off the land and sea, children have little incentive to leave their communities for higher education and other careers.

Many Native Alaskans also harbor deep suspicions about outsiders who pledge to help them, believing they will join a long line of *cheechakos* (a Chinook term for Alaskan newcomers who are more interested in exploiting the state's natural resources than assimilating with natives). Thus, the first test of Project GRAD's expansion into Alaska will be how well organizers understand and respond to the historical context for change in the Kenai Peninsula Schools.

"We can't do the program the way we typically do it here," said Robert Rivera, executive director of Project GRAD–USA. "I think we'll find out a whole lot more [in coming months] how we'll have to adjust the components. I don't think we know fully what it's going to mean yet. . . . We don't know if we can pull it off."

Such frank talk about the organization's ability to serve all schools well represents a shift in thinking for Project GRAD. Executives now openly acknowledge having to make many adjustments as the organization matures. A decade into the process of trying to transform the education of impoverished students, Project GRAD has realized that it can no longer ride into town like a knight determined to rescue besieged castles. Each community has something to offer as well as something to improve. When working with prospective school districts, Project GRAD now signals its desire to learn, not just to teach.

"I do believe we may not be the answer to every troubled school district, and we need to define our niche," said Stephanie Smith-Arce of Project GRAD–USA. "I think we recognize that there are issues in each city. What we're trying to do is provide as much support and model how the program should be implemented. It can't be a coercive measure. It has to be about education and ensuring a vehicle for communicating best practices across the network."

Ironically, Project GRAD's willingness to adjust its programs and practices to fit local conditions is what drew the Kenai Peninsula schools to the organization, just as Project GRAD's reluctance to accommodate alienated some districts in earlier negotiations. The tension between maintaining fidelity to the model while offering flexibility to each community puts constant pressure on Project GRAD, which must hold school districts accountable for results yet help them respond to distinctive challenges.

Dr. Donna Peterson, superintendent of the Kenai Peninsula Borough School District, said she and the members of her leadership team tend to be skeptical about education vendors, believing that few of them have the data to support their claims or the ability to tailor their products. She stated, "We're very careful about what programs get inside of our boundaries. . . . If it doesn't pass our test of what would work tomorrow in a first grade classroom, it isn't going anywhere. And ninety percent of the flash-in-the-pan stuff doesn't."

After hearing about Project GRAD from U.S. senator Ted Stevens of Alaska, chairman of the Senate Appropriations Committee, Kenai Peninsula administrators spent time in Houston observing Project GRAD schools

and analyzing the group's research. Peterson and her team had already identified common problems in the district's low-performing schools, including
excessive teacher turnover, inconsistent curricula, and limited involvement
from parents. At first, the district considered addressing the issues individually by using separate strategies or programs. Then administrators realized
that Project GRAD offered a way to resolve them comprehensively.

Peterson said the decision to form a partnership with Project GRAD
hinged on the organization's willingness to listen to the school district's
concerns and commit to staying in Alaska for at least 12 years.

"There were several places here that Project GRAD might not have
made it. Had they acted differently, we would have said, 'Thank you for
your ideas but we're going to have to tell you this isn't for us,'" said Peterson. "GRAD understands our unique needs. They don't even blink anymore when we say, 'But what about . . . ?'"

During the 2-year process of negotiations with the Kenai Peninsula
schools, Project GRAD kept searching for solutions that were specific to
the region. For example, Project GRAD brought representatives from the
Alaskan ethnic communities to Houston to teach the national organization
about their cultural traditions. Teresa Standifer, mother of three children at
Tebughna Elementary School, is one of those who made the trip. She said
she discussed her mixed experiences with school, including the low academic standards that forced her to send her oldest daughter away to boarding school in the 9th grade and the lack of social preparation that caused
Standifer to abandon her own dream of becoming a certified teacher. After
graduating from Tebughna, Standifer had accepted a full scholarship to
Alaska Pacific University in Anchorage, but she returned home after only
a week on her own. "I got there and froze," she said. "Nobody had ever
taken me out of the community and told me what college would be like."

Standifer believes Tebughna is "taking the right step" in partnering
with Project GRAD. The consistent curricular features that Project GRAD
offers will be especially welcome after the 90 minutes of daily "choice
time" that one of her son's former teachers permitted, she noted. By contrast, Standifer said, veteran teacher Don Torres helped the same child advance two grade levels the following year at Tebughna, which she believes
demonstrates the difference that dedicated and experienced educators can
make in a child's education.

Another local adaptation Project GRAD plans for the Kenai Peninsula is condensing the college preparatory institutes to 2 weeks instead of 4 because many families can't afford to lose a month of their children's help on commercial fishing operations. Likewise, Project GRAD reconfigured the typical house-to-house Walk for Success—where families sign contracts agreeing to abide by the terms of the scholarship agreement—to village gatherings where parents can learn about the program in one central location. Project GRAD also plans to use videoconferences and other distance learning strategies to ensure that teachers in isolated communities can participate in timely professional development activities.

"WE NEED TO WORK *WITH* THEM"

One of the most visible signs of Project GRAD's greater consideration of local needs is the recruitment of Bob Moore to lead the Project GRAD–Kenai Peninsula board of directors. Although neither a Native Alaskan nor an Old Believer, Moore has strong credibility within the various communities. His record of bridging cultural divides serves as a model of how outsiders can form strong partnerships with local residents to improve education.

Moore and his wife moved to the Kenai Peninsula from Tennessee in 1969, the same year that five families of Old Believers bought a one-square-mile tract of land from the state and built the village of Nikolaevsk. At the time, the remote property had no direct access to a paved road. So Moore would park his car several miles away and hike, ski, or snowshoe through the fields and over a narrow river to the trailer that the Kenai Peninsula district had set up as the town's school. The first teacher hired by the district spoke fluent Russian but didn't come to work on a regular basis and lasted only a few months. When Moore arrived to start the 1970–71 school year, none of the 19 students he expected to teach in the 1st through 8th grades had shown up for class.

Undaunted, Moore found a 10-year-old boy who spoke English and asked him to translate as the teacher walked house to house to introduce himself to parents. Although Moore promised to respect the group's cultural traditions, the village elders had doubts. For several months, he said, one or more elders showed up each day to observe silently from the back of the classroom. By November, however, Nikolaevsk School enrolled 43 students and the elders had stopped monitoring Moore's instruction.

In Moore's second year, the school district hired another teacher and a Russian-speaking teacher's aide to keep up with Nikolaevsk's burgeoning enrollment. Using lumber and other materials that an oil company had donated to the school district, village residents built two permanent classrooms to replace the trailer. Patiently and faithfully, public education gained a firm foundation in Nikolaevsk.

In September 1975, Moore arrived one morning and found five men waiting for him at the entrance to the school. Wondering if he had done something to offend them, he invited them inside. Instead of finding fault with his teaching, however, they asked if he would help them become citizens of the United States.

Moore obtained some instructional materials from the U.S. Immigration and Naturalization Service and asked the men to bring any interested adults to an evening meeting at the school. When 65 people showed up that night, Moore volunteered to teach a 3-hour citizenship course twice a week in addition to his regular workload. Six months later, 59 of those people passed the citizenship test on a single day. A few years later, Moore taught a similar course and helped 86 Old Believers become citizens. Other groups followed in subsequent years.

The pattern of respectful accommodation and assistance continued. When Moore—who had become the school's principal in addition to its lead teacher—wanted to add a high school to the elementary grades, he asked the village elders instead of demanding their compliance. He told the community's leaders that children were leaving school after 8th grade, usually at age 14 or 15, but the state required them to attend classes until they were 16.

"I said, 'We're breaking the law. I don't want to break the law. What can we do?' They said, 'Mr. Moore, we will talk.'"

At the end of their regular weekend church services, the Old Believers traditionally discuss any civic issues in a town meeting format. On this particular day, the main topic was the future of the village school. The following Monday, the village elders returned to share the results of their forum with the principal.

"Mr. Moore, this is easy," they told him. "You just add one more year of school."

By presenting the situation as a problem they could jointly solve, Moore gave community members a voice in a decision that affected them. This method enabled people who had a history of being abused by authorities to view educators in a positive light. In addition, by respecting the greater time that the village elders needed to reach a decision, Moore paved the way for future collaborations. During his 23 years as a teacher and principal at Nikolaevsk, he persuaded the community to expand to a comprehensive high school, add a full-day kindergarten, and let children play competitive sports. He also helped the first girl from the village go away to college.

"I would guess that, conservatively, I talked to her family, her father and mother, sixty hours to persuade them to let her go," Moore said, adding that one of the biggest fears in the community to this day is that the students will leave the village and lose their religion. "I said, 'I know this girl's character. I've worked with her all these years. She was captain of the basketball team. She was editor of the newspaper. She helped write literature and books that we published in our school in both languages. I don't think she'll lose'" her faith traditions.

The student eventually graduated from the University of Oregon with a bachelor's degree in Russian, Moore said, and she later earned a master's degree in education. She now teaches near an Old Believers' community in Oregon and still practices the faith.

Although he retired from Nikolaevsk in 1993, Moore visits the community on a regular basis. He also worked as a substitute principal in three other Kenai Peninsula schools that will become part of Project GRAD and maintains close contact with community members of all ages.

"Everybody trusts him," said Rick Matiya, who was the first school administrator in Razdolna and Voznesenka, two of the Old Believers' communities that will participate in Project GRAD. "I would always use Bob to help filter and understand how they're thinking in Razdolna and Voznesenka. . . . He knows them all."

Moore also serves on the board of a community college in Homer, Alaska, where some of the women who are Old Believers come to complete high school equivalency exams and take classes leading to associate's degrees. Moore is one of their biggest cheerleaders, persuading the women that at the very least they must be able to support their families if their husbands die or become disabled, a not-uncommon occurrence in the commercial fishing industry.

Although he remains hopeful that the children of his former students will attend college in greater numbers than their parents and grandparents did, Moore knows that the Old Believers adapt slowly. For example, after Project GRAD's public announcement at Nikolaevsk in September 2003, a group of girls huddled around a 15-year-old classmate as she discussed plans for her upcoming wedding ceremony. Some of the teenagers said they intend to go to college, but others expressed no interest. Changing their views will require patience and persistence on the part of Project GRAD.

"That's one of my fears with Project GRAD, that they might come in and try to 'fix'" all the schools without understanding their history, Moore said. "That's why I'm involved, bottom line. I don't want somebody going in and *'fixing'* the native community or *'fixing'* the Old Believer community. We need to work *with* them. They are stubborn. They are hard headed. And I am, too."

COPING WITH CHANGING TIMES

Throughout the 1970s and 1980s, there was little economic incentive for Alaskan youths to go to college. Before the state imposed quotas to protect depleted natural resources, commercial fishermen in the Kenai Peninsula routinely earned more than $100,000 a year, which they often invested in larger fleets. Massive public construction projects and oil and gas pipeline installation also brought high wages to people with limited formal education. But as the state's economic boom shrank during the 1990s, so did the employment options for those without high school diplomas and college degrees.

Just as older generations have had to cope with changing employment patterns in other areas of the country dominated by faded industries, parents in Alaska are trying to figure out how the recent economic changes will affect their children's future. Families who never dreamed that their children would need or want to attend college now must consider how to prepare for a range of new possibilities, from paying tuition to finding a university that will support their religious faith. Some remain skeptical that a college education is necessary for their children.

"I make more money than [college-educated] engineers on the same project," boasted one heavy equipment operator whose son is among the first students who were promised college scholarships through Project GRAD. "Education is good, but it doesn't necessarily guarantee success."

Other parents acknowledge that their children will have to overcome many barriers before making a smooth transition to college. For those who belong to communities of Old Believers, the process will include finding a college that will let them worship on 12 major religious holidays during the year and attend regular church services. These parents said they are hopeful that Project GRAD will work with them to prepare their children for college while also honoring their religious values.

Whether they are Old Believers, Native Alaskans, or Latino immigrants, parents of first-generation college students often fear that their children will fail to maintain strong ties to the communities that raised them. If they accept the notion that their children may not follow in their footsteps, parents at least want assurance that their children won't reject everything they stand for. Any organization seeking to change the future of disadvantaged students must therefore understand the importance that their families place on cultural preservation.

Such emotional issues affect all school reform initiatives aimed at impoverished populations, and they can ultimately undercut the outside supports provided to students. As difficult as it may be to address these factors, reformers ignore them at their peril. Raising money for programs and scholarships, providing targeted training to teachers, and guiding and mentoring students—all of these needs must be handled with precision and care. But one of the most difficult tasks for those who hope to raise achievement in low-performing schools will always be winning the hearts and minds of people.

"I had plans to move until I heard about Project GRAD," said Connie Burnell, whose children attend Tebughna Elementary in Tyonek, Alaska. "It gave me hope. I decided to stay and see."

Chapter 10

THE SYSTEM AND THE STUDENT

An estimated 8,000 U.S. schools spend in excess of $1 billion a year on about 300 different education reform models and methods (Colgan, 2001). Poor, urban schools represent a significant portion of those seeking to change their current circumstances. State, local, and federal governments, individual philanthropists, and national and regional foundations have invested billions of dollars in urban school reform initiatives that have attained mostly disappointing and short-term results. Studies of the New American Schools, the Edna McConnell Clark Foundation's Program for Student Achievement, the Annenberg Challenge, the Annie E. Casey Foundation's "New Futures" effort, the Pew Foundation's "Children's Initiative," and other reform efforts have concluded that the schools they assisted often failed to make or sustain expected improvements (Center on Reinventing Public Education, 2002; Annenberg Institute for School Reform, 2003; Campbell, Harvey, & DeArmond, 2001; Edna McConnell Clark Foundation, 2003; Thomas B. Fordham Foundation, 2001; see also Viadero, 2002). Charter schools and voucher programs, which other groups have touted as remedies for students mired in low-achieving communities, have also had limited success (Brownstein, 2001).

"It is sobering, but not terribly surprising, that the challenge has grown more rather than less complex with the accumulation of knowledge and experience," Marla Ucelli (2001) concluded in a paper prepared for the Rockefeller Foundation. "Leveraging change that will truly produce greater equity in access to high-quality teaching and learning requires action on the demand and supply sides. It requires time, resources, perseverance, and truth telling. It requires using well the hard-won knowledge of reformers and funders alike" (p. 15).

While success remains elusive or incremental, urban reform initiatives continue to attract followers and interest. Such is the depth of the problems in impoverished communities and such is the degree of optimism that we can eventually fix them. Yet rarely do the reforms include all of the complementary components that research and experience have shown to be effective in raising achievement levels among disadvantaged populations. These include ongoing, job-embedded professional development for teachers, which enables them to create consistent, high-quality, and engaging lessons for students; culturally sensitive and inclusive methods of involving families in their children's education; mentoring, guidance, and interventions for students as they reach beyond their limited horizons; and the commitment and resources necessary to carry the plans through to completion.

As Patricia A. Wasley (2003), dean of the College of Education at the University of Washington, notes: "Since I began my education career, many approaches have been initiated to close the gap in achievement between kids of color—mainly Black, Latino, and Native American kids—and their higher-achieving counterparts. During the 1960s, we tried to create more relevant curricula, bused kids to integrate schools, and experimented with open classrooms. In the 1970s, we implemented instructional leadership; tried curriculum mapping; developed multicultural curricula; raised teacher expectations, particularly for girls; adopted students' learning objectives; and applied lessons from 'effective schools.' In the 1980s we worked on high school reform, performance assessment, outcomes-based education, and site-based decision-making. And, in the 1990s, we developed standards at the local/district, state, and federal levels in all the disciplines and began the work of building high-stakes accountability.

"Given all the effort, and America's 'can-do' reputation, one might wonder why we haven't managed to close the gap by now. The answer is not so hard to divine: There has never been universal agreement about equal opportunity for kids of color. If there were, we would not waste our time and resources on simplistic solutions" (pp. 12–13).

Closing the achievement gap for poor and minority students is such a complex task that no singularly directed effort could ever hope to succeed. A new report by the Educational Testing Service of Princeton, New Jersey, has identified a set of 14 factors that strongly affect educational achievement for disadvantaged populations. These include school-specific issues, such as the rigor of the curriculum, class size, and teacher experience and attendance; as well as contributing causes outside of schools, such as children's birth weights, lead poisoning, television watching, and parent availability. The study's author found racial and ethnic gaps in all of the indicators of student success, and socioeconomic gaps on 11 of the 14 factors (Educational Testing Service, 2003). Realistically, then, all of these problems must be addressed if we hope to turn the tide.

Decades of reform have taught us that rehabilitating low-performing schools is an intricate and laborious process that depends on strong public-private partnerships; targeted strategies for improving teaching and learning; extensive academic and emotional supports for students; and significant financial resources to ensure that schools have the resources and remedies to sustain reform. That's the global picture. But efforts to improve urban education must also address the needs of thousands of individuals who have to be specifically and collectively persuaded to change.

By design, Project GRAD understands that raising achievement in schools that have been slowed by decades of poverty, neglect, and low expectations requires a sophisticated plan for supporting children as they move from kindergarten through high school. An increasingly strong organizational and programmatic scaffold is helping children in Project GRAD schools learn to climb the academic ladder. But weak relationships anywhere can still cause them to fall. Promising a future to children who don't believe they have one must include strategies for guiding every child, every grade level, every year. And if the goal is a college degree, the supports can't stop after high school.

Dr. Joseph Kahne, director of the doctoral program in educational leadership at Mills College in Oakland, California, has studied some of the formal efforts to get greater numbers of disadvantaged students to college, including Eugene Lang's "I Have a Dream" program. So many factors influence a child's future, Kahne said, that it can be very difficult to determine which carried the most weight. Nevertheless, he said, it's impossible to ignore the fact that successful interventions invariably include sustained, intimate relationships between children and adult advocates.

"On a lot of levels, there's evidence that it is through long-term, committed relationships that kids get the support that allows them to negotiate the things that are thrown at them throughout their lives," Kahne said. "One year, it's a problem with gangs. Another year, something horrible happens to their family and they have to move. Another year, there's a real conflict with the math teacher. Whatever it is, these problems are constant and they are changing. The way that kids negotiate these is through having someone to help. Of course, there are always some kids who get through without help, and that's why some of them survive in the worst situations. But most of us need help."

Any initiative that aims to improve conditions for students in chaotic urban settings must understand the importance of maintaining close relationships with the youths, Kahne said. School bureaucracies aren't equipped to provide those personal links because they apportion resources and manage programs collectively, not individually. Even when districts employ people to interact with disadvantaged families, he said, they typically don't have the means to follow those families as they move in and out of particular schools.

"The difference in sending someone to your house who's known you and your family for four years and . . . doesn't pronounce your name differently is night and day," Kahne said. "In many urban settings, thirty to fifty percent of the kids change every year. There's such chaos and ripping away of relationships. But when you know them and you knew their older brother, that's invaluable in building trust and understanding.

"If the economic payoff of getting an education were enough to convince kids to go to college, they wouldn't need anything else, because the incentive is already built into the system. We know there is an economic incentive to stay in school. The problem is that kids can't look five years down the road to the economic payoff. It's too distant, it's too remote, and it isn't about trust and understanding. It's invaluable that financial aid enables kids to go to college, but it's nowhere near sufficient."

BELIEVING IN THEIR POTENTIAL

After 10 years in Houston and 6 or fewer years in other cities, Project GRAD is still a work-in-progress, with both successes and failures marking its path. Yet it's impossible to discount the impact of a reform that has placed thousands of impoverished students on college campuses that they probably would not have seen up close except for the view behind a mop or a rake. At a time when experts predict that rapidly rising tuition costs will lead to the first decline in high school graduates enrolling in college since World War II (Pitsch, 2003), students in Project GRAD schools continue surpassing rates typical for schools serving high-poverty communities. Although some Project GRAD students struggle in college and drop out before completing degrees, they no longer consider higher education an unattainable or unaffordable goal. Nor do they believe that temporary setbacks will permanently close off their options.

Consider the experiences of Mercy Donohue, a Project GRAD scholar from Houston. Before enrolling in Davis High School during the 1997–98 school year, Mercy had lived in five states and attended two other high schools. Her parents struggled financially and emotionally, and when they divorced, Mercy and her pregnant mother moved to Texas to live with an aunt and her four children in a crowded Houston duplex. The newcomers slept on the floor. Mercy often studied by porch light. "It was crazy and no real privacy," she said. "I had to stay up after they went to sleep to do my homework because I had to take care of them before then."

Teachers at Davis came to the rescue. They opened their classrooms and homes after hours. They encouraged her to get involved in extracurricular activities, and she often stayed at school into the evening so she could get away from family traumas. She joined the student council, the tennis and golf teams, and she and her debate team partner became the first Davis students to qualify for the state finals during her junior year. She also worked with business mentors who came to Davis on a regular basis, persuading her that she should give college a try.

Mercy said, "There was always somebody from Project GRAD coming into the school or sitting down and talking to us. It was really nice to let us know that there were businesspeople who were concerned about what we were doing and what we were thinking, that we were important. . . . It wasn't just my parents and people who knew me who said that but somebody I didn't have any connection to, just people who thought I had potential."

Her sophomore English teacher, Amanda McDonald, provided inspiration and concern that went way beyond the call of duty. After McDonald praised one of the first short stories she wrote for class, Mercy started staying behind at the end of the school day to seek her teacher's counsel. Later,

McDonald hired Mercy to babysit her daughter, and she often stayed the entire weekend at McDonald's home. At one point, she moved in with McDonald when the difficulties with her own family became overwhelming.

"Any lesser of a kid would have given up. . . . She's had a lot to deal with," said McDonald, who currently teaches at Lee High School in Houston. "There was something about her that caused people to reach out to her."

Mercy signed up for Project GRAD at the end of her sophomore year and attended the summer institute at the University of Houston-Downtown. After her junior year, she earned a spot at the Cornell summer institute along with 10 other students from Davis. Because of the large number of students attending the Cornell session that year, Mercy had to raise most of the $6,000 tuition herself. She used a scholarship from the Houston City Breakfast Club and plenty of sweat equity from car washes, lawn work, barbecues, and babysitting. Being at an Ivy League university made the hard work and sacrifices worth the struggle, she said. "I loved it," she said of the summer institute. "Ohmygod, I can't believe I'm doing this. I'm researching. I'm editing papers. That's when I was sure I was going to college, no matter what."

Back at Davis, Mercy noticed differences between the students who had attended the Cornell institute and those who had stayed in Houston. When teachers tried to raise the academic standards in class during her senior year, she said, the students who hadn't gone away for the summer complained, which caused some teachers to relent. By contrast, the students who had challenged themselves at Cornell knew they needed rigorous assignments if they wanted to succeed in college.

"We have had conversations about how it would have helped a lot to have had better preparation" at Davis, she said. "But I don't know how to do that when some of the students already flat out won't do homework."

Mercy graduated from Davis in the spring of 2000 and entered Colgate University in the fall. She turned down offers to attend several state universities, and she rejected a full scholarship to Knox College in Illinois because she believed Colgate had a better psychology department. She took out some loans (she will have to repay a total of about $15,000 by the time she earns her bachelor's degree) and used grants and a part-time job to pay for what her scholarships didn't cover at Colgate.

Money proved to be one of many obstacles in college. Emotional and academic strains also took a toll. Three of Mercy's freshman roommates had come from elite boarding schools and another had graduated from a private high school. Their parents gave them generous personal spending accounts that enabled them to take weekend trips and buy whatever they wanted while in college.

Mercy felt inferior from the start. She recalled a conversation during the first week of school when her roommates inquired about each other's backgrounds and their scores on the college entrance exams. Mercy demurred on the latter question, but when she confided that she had attended a high school in "inner-city Houston," one of her roommates made her weaker credentials a patronizing reference point throughout the year.

Mercy said she didn't want the offensive roommate or anyone else to believe that Colgate had admitted her only because she was a minority. She purposely sought a diverse circle of friends instead of joining the Latin American Student Organization or fraternizing only with people from disadvantaged backgrounds. Nevertheless, she became increasingly self-conscious. Although it had never bothered her before to wear her cousin's hand-me-downs or to shop for clothes at Wal-Mart, she now noticed that other students always had access to the latest fashions and didn't have to work while in school.

In addition to the economic and ethnic disparities, Mercy realized she didn't know how to study well like her peers. She fell so far behind in a sociology class during the first semester that she went to speak with the professor. Mercy offered to write additional papers to compensate for her low grades, saying that she understood the material but was having a difficult time with the test format. Her professor would not oblige.

Mercy ended up passing the sociology class with a D, but it was only one of many crises averted. She found some satisfaction in her part-time job as a campus secretary, where she earned money for books, plane tickets, and other expenses. However, she said, "There are still times when the money gets to me and I think that I should go back to Houston and work as a secretary for fifteen dollars an hour."

She rebounded from her difficult freshman year, earning a 3.5 grade-point average during her sophomore year. As a junior, she suffered from stomach ulcers and a hiatal hernia and was bed-ridden for several weeks during the first semester. She took a medical leave from her classes but resumed her studies the following semester. She said she fought to remain at Colgate during her recovery because she feared that if she returned home to live, however briefly, she would be sucked into the vortex of the family's ongoing crises and would not return to college.

"I was explaining to one of my professors, 'Don't send me back home. I am my family's retirement,'" Mercy said. "If you're a first-generation (student) and try to go to a good college, you can't stay in the same city or state. The influences that the family has over you are so strong. Everything you go through, they go through."

She points to one of her cousins who earned a Project GRAD scholarship after graduating from Davis High School but who chose to live at home while attending a local college. The cousin dropped out of school after a year.

Mercy bolstered her resolve to stay in college by communicating with peers from Davis and by touching base with her high school mentors whenever she visited Houston. These advocates understand her, she said. They help her focus on the future when so many current problems make it seem easier to give up the fight.

Mercy is on target to graduate from Colgate in December 2004 with a bachelor's degree in women's studies and a minor in psychology. She is investigating master's level and doctoral programs in forensics psychology because she believes she will need advanced degrees to get ahead in her intended career. "I have a goal, and I'm trying to say I'm going to reach that," she said. "I'm stubborn, and I think it helps."

That same determination to move past adversity characterizes Project GRAD's work in America's weakest public schools. Helping students develop resiliency while providing long-term academic, emotional, and financial supports might be the best measure of success in Project GRAD schools. Like Mercy Donohue, Project GRAD might stumble from time to time, might have to work harder than others to get ahead, but neither the organization nor its scholars have been willing to quit without a fight. Both are committed to excelling—whatever it takes.

NOTES

INTRODUCTION

1. In 2003, a state audit alleged that the Houston Independent School District (HISD) substantially undercounted high school dropouts. During the 2000–01 school year, for example, school officials lacked sufficient evidence that 3,000 of 5,500 missing students were continuing their education elsewhere. Project GRAD conducted its own investigation of Davis High School dropouts, comparing incoming 9th graders with the number of graduates 4 years later and tracking individual students to see whether they transferred to other schools, completed high school equivalency exams, or left school altogether. Project GRAD's calculations revealed that 24% of the Davis High School class of 2001 dropped out, for example, compared to the 6.8% rate for Davis that HISD reported to the state. Nationwide, according to U.S. Census figures, Latinos account for about 16% of 16- to 19-year-olds, but nearly 34% of the dropouts.

2. To put the Davis students' successes in perspective, consider that only 3% of students at the nation's most selective colleges come from families whose incomes fall in the bottom one fourth of wage earners. Despite complaints that affirmative-action policies at many U.S. colleges pass over qualified white applicants in favor of less-qualified minority candidates to reach campus diversity goals, it is still highly unusual for poor students, including immigrants, to gain admission to top universities. See Holmes, S. A., & Winter, G. (2003, June 29). Fixing the race gap in 25 years or less. *The New York Times*, Sec. 4, pp. 1, 14.

3. Unless otherwise indicated, all quotations that are not attributed to books or periodicals came from direct interviews with the author.

CHAPTER 1

1. The total societal cost for one career criminal is estimated at $1.5 to $1.8 million, which represents 25% for victim costs, 50% for lost quality of life, 20% for criminal justice expenses, and 5% for lost productivity. See Cohen, 1998, p.

17. In addition, high school dropouts represent nearly half of the nation's heads of household on welfare and nearly half of the nation's prison population. See Kollars, D. (1998, September 6). When many kids drop out, state loses track [Electronic version]. *Sacramento Bee*. Retrieved from http://www.sacbee.com/news/projects/nobodys_kids/index. html.

CHAPTER 5

1. Chapter title taken from H. Jerome Freiberg (1996, September). From tourists to citizens in the classroom. *Educational Leadership*, *54*(1), 32–36.

2. Although classroom managers play an important part in the process of teaching students how to accept greater responsibility for their learning, Freiberg noted that there are more than 100 other elements that comprise CMCD.

CHAPTER 6

1. Schools in some of the expansion cities that joined the Project GRAD network after Houston chose to continue using the math curricula they already had in place. In addition, not all middle schools adopted MOVE IT Math when Project GRAD expanded the program into the middle grades.

2. At the start of the 2002–03 school year, HISD merged Lamar and nearby Lee elementary schools into a new building named after Jim Ketelsen, with Lamar Principal Alma Lara in charge.

CHAPTER 8

1. Central High School, which the district closed in 1997 and reopened in 1999, joined Project GRAD in the fall of 2000, more than 2 years later than Shabazz. The first group of Project GRAD scholars from Central will graduate in 2004.

2. Dr. George Brumley, his wife, Jean Stanback Brumley, and 10 family members died in a plane crash in Kenya in the summer of 2003. He was 68. The entire Brumley family was well known in Atlanta for its philanthropic efforts on the part of public health, education, and the arts.

REFERENCES

Academic excellence indicator system 1994 campus report. (1995). [Marshall Middle School data file, retrieved Oct. 12, 2003 from http://www.tea.state.tx.us.] Austin, TX: Texas Education Agency.

Adelman, C. (1999). *Answers in the toolbox: Academic intensity, attendance patterns, and bachelor's degree attainment.* Washington, DC: U.S. Department of Education.

Agnew, K. C. (2001). *Staff development for school reform: A case study of the Consistency Management & Cooperative Discipline® Model* (Doctoral dissertation, University of Houston). *Dissertation Abstracts International* (UMI No. 3003139)

Alaska Natives Commission. (1994). *Alaska native education, report of the Education Task Force final report, 1*(4). Retrieved Aug. 10, 2003 from http://www.alaskool.org.resources/anc2/ANC2.

Alexander, D., Heaviside, S., & Farris, E. (1999). *Status of education reform in public elementary and secondary schools: Teachers' perspective.* Washington, DC: National Center for Education Statistics.

American Council on Education (2003). *Minorities in higher education annual status report* [Electronic version]. Retrieved Jan. 27, 2004 from http://www.acenet.edu/news/press_release/2003/10october/minority_report.cfm.

American Federation of Teachers. (1998a, January). *Building on the best, learning from what works: Seven promising reading and English Language Arts programs.* Washington, DC: Author.

American Federation of Teachers. (1998b, July). *Building on the best, learning from what works: Six promising schoolwide reform programs.* Washington, DC: Author.

American Federation of Teachers. (2000, July). *Building on the best, learning from what works: Five promising discipline and violence prevention programs.* Washington, DC: Author.

Annenberg Institute for School Reform. (2003, March). *Research perspectives on school reform: Lessons from the Annenberg challenge.* Providence, RI: Author.

Bacon, P. (2003, June 25). Urban kids struggle with AP [Electronic version]. *Time.* Retrieved July 8, 2003 from http://www.time.com/time/nation/article/0,8599,460610,00.html.

Balfanz, R., & Legters, N. (2001). *How many Central City high schools have a severe dropout problem, where are they located, and who attends them? Estimates using the common core of data.* Retrieved June 17, 2003 from the Civil Rights Project at Harvard University, http://www.gse.harvard.edu/research/dropouts/call_dropoutpapers.php.

Balfanz, R., & Legters, N. (2004, June). *Locating the dropout crises: Which high schools produce the nation's dropouts? Where are they located? Who attends them?* Baltimore, MD: Johns Hopkins University Center for Social Organization of Schools.

Barthe, P. (2000, Spring). Honor in the boxcar: Equalizing teacher quality. *Thinking K-16, 4*(1), 10–11.

Bell-Rose, S., Chaplin, D., Hannaway, J., & Creaturo, S. (1998). *African American high scorers project, technical report three: Student activities, course taking, school performance, and SAT performance.* New York: Andrew W. Mellon Foundation.

Borman, G. D., Hewes, G. M., Overman, L. T. & Brown, S. (2002, November). *Comprehensive school reform and student achievement: A meta-analysis.* Baltimore, MD: Center for Research on the Education of Students Placed At Risk, Johns Hopkins University.

Borman, G. D., & Hewes, G. M. (2003). The long-term effects and cost-effectiveness of Success for All. *Educational Evaluation and Policy Analysis, 24,* 243–266.

Bradach, J. (2003, Spring). Going to scale: The challenge of replicating social programs. *Stanford Social Innovation Review, 1*(1), 24–25.

Brophy, B. A. (2001, Spring). Powerful allies. *Ford Foundation Report,* p. 31.

Brownstein, R. (2001, December 17). A lesson for congress: No school reform quick fix. *Los Angeles Times,* p. A18.

Campbell, C., Harvey, J., & DeArmond, M. (2001, April 18). RAND finds mixed results of school reform models. *Education Week,* p. 7.

Carnevale, A. P., & Fry, R. A. (2000). *Crossing the great divide: Can we achieve equity when generation Y goes to college?* Princeton, NJ: Educational Testing Service.

Cavanagh, S. (2002, October 2). College-attendance racial gap narrowed in 1990s, study says. *Education Week,* p. 11.

Cavanagh, S. (2003, March 5). Oregon study outlines standards for college preparedness. *Education Week,* p. 6.

Center on Reinventing Public Education. (2002, August). *Philanthropic due diligence: Exploratory case studies to improve investments in urban schools.* Seattle, WA: Author.

Chase, B. (2000, February 7). Literacy alert: At home or school, never take reading for granted. Column retrieved on Oct. 13, 2003 from http://www.nea. org/columns/bc000227.html.

Coalition for Juvenile Justice. (2001). *Abandoned in the back row: New lessons in education and delinquency prevention* (2001 Annual Report). Washington, DC: Author.

Coffey, E., & Lashway, L. (2002, October 21). *Trends and issues: School reform* [Electronic version]. Eugene, OR: Clearinghouse on Educational Policy and Management. (ERIC Digest). Retrieved on March 22, 2002 from http://eric. uoregon.edu/trends_issues/reform/index.html.

Cohen, M. A. (1998). The monetary value of saving a high-risk youth. *Journal of Quantitative Criminology, 14*(1), 17.

Colgan, C. (2001, December 18). To succeed, reform models require long-term commitment. *School Board News*, p. 8.

Council of the Great City Schools. (2001, March). *A decade of ACT results in the nation's urban schools 1990–1999: A report on urban student achievement and course taking.* Washington, DC: Author.

Cunningham, A., Redmond, C., & Merisotis, J. (2003). *Investing early: Intervention programs in selected U.S. states.* Washington, DC: Institute for Higher Education Policy and the Canadian Millennium Scholarship Foundation.

Darling-Hammond, L., & Youngs, P. (2002, December). Defining "highly qualified teachers": What does "scientifically-based research" actually tell us? *Education Researcher, 31*(9), 22.

Dillon, J. (2003, September 7). Project GRAD Kenai Peninsula gets warm reception for the most part. *Peninsula Clarion*, p. 1. Retrieved Sept. 7, 2003 from http://www.msnbc.com/local/kpc/N090703new001001.asp.

Edna McConnell Clark Foundation. (2003). *Standards-based middle grades reform in six urban districts, 1995–2001: A report on the program for student achievement of the Edna McConnell Clark Foundation.* New York: Anne Mackinnon.

Education Week. (1998, January 8). Quarter-century quagmire. *Quality Counts '98: The Urban Challenge, XVII*(17), 205.

Educational Testing Service. (2003, October). *Parsing the achievement gap: Baselines for tracking progress.* Princeton, NJ: Paul E. Barton.

Elmore, R. F. (2002, September-October). Testing trap [Electronic version]. *Harvard Magazine, 105*(1), 35. Retrieved Jan. 28, 2004 from http://www.harvard-Magazine.com/on-lin/0902140.html.

The Evaluation and Training Institute. (2002, July). *Evaluation of teacher outcomes (Final report submitted to Project GRAD–Los Angeles)*. Los Angeles, CA: Author.

Freedman, M. (1991, Fall). *The kindness of strangers: Reflections on the mentoring movement*. Philadelphia: Public/Private Ventures.

Freiberg, H. J. (2002, May 2–3). Preventing classroom problems before they begin. Consistency Management & Cooperative Discipline® state-wide conference. Houston, TX: University of Houston.

Fry, R. (2002). *Latinos in higher education: Many enroll, too few graduate*. Washington, DC: Pew Hispanic Center.

Fry, R. (2004, June 23). *Latino youth finishing college: The role of selective pathways*. Washington, DC: Pew Hispanic Center.

Gaustad, J. (1992, December). *School discipline* (Report No. 78). Eugene, OR: University of Oregon Clearinghouse on Educational Management. (ERIC Document Reproduction Service No. ED3500727).

Gewertz, C. (2002, October 16). Trusting school community linked to student gains. *Education Week, 22*(7), 8.

Gewertz, C. (2004, March 31). Urban students show reading, math gains on state assessments. *Education Week, 23*(29), 10.

Gold, E., Simon, E., & Brown, C. (2002). *Strong neighborhoods strong schools: The indicators project on education organizing*. Chicago: Cross City Campaign for Urban School Reform.

Greene, J. P. (2002, April). *High school graduation rates in the United States*. New York: Manhattan Institute for Policy Research.

Greene, J. P., & Forster, G. (2003, September). *Public high school graduation and college readiness rates in the United States (Education Working Paper No. 3)*. New York: Manhattan Institute.

Groff, P. (2003). [Review of the book *Success for all: Research and reform in elementary education*]. *Teachers College Record, 105*(1). Retrieved May 29, 2002 from http://www.tcrecord.org/Content.asp?ContentID=10929.

Haberman, M. (1991, December). The pedagogy of poverty versus good teaching [Electronic version]. *Phi Delta Kappan, 73*(4), 290–294. Retrieved Sept. 2, 2002 from http://www.enc.org/topics/equity/articles/document.shtm?input=ACQ-111376-1376.

Ham, S., Doolittle, F. C., & Holton, G. I. (2000, August). *Building the foundation for improved student performance: The pre-curricular phase of Project GRAD Newark*. New York: MDRC.

Hill, D. (1998, August/September). Success story. *Teacher, 10*(3), 46–49.

Hodge, S. (2001, January 14). Getting smart about education: Retired executive devotes energy to launching and maintaining stay-in-school program [Electronic version]. *Houston chronicle*, Lifestyle p. 2. Retrieved June 13, 2003 from http://www.chron.com.

Holmes, S. A., & Winter, G. (2003, June 29). Fixing the race gap in 25 years or less. *New York Times*, sec. 4, pp. 1, 14.

Horn, L., Wei, C. C., & Berker, A. (2002). *What students pay for college: Changes in net price of college attendance between 1992–93 and 1999–2000* (NCES 2002174). [Electronic version] Washington, DC: National Center for Education Statistics. Retrieved Jan. 16, 2003 from http://nces.ed.gov/das/epubs/2002174/index.asp.

James, D. W. (2001). *Raising minority academic achievement: A compendium of education programs and practices.* Washington, DC: American Youth Policy Forum.

Jehl, J., Blank, M. J., & McCloud, B. (2001, April 5). *Ensuring a positive future for children and youth: Bridging the work of educators and community builders.* Washington, DC: Institute for Educational Leadership.

Joftus, S. (2002, September). *Every child a graduate: A framework for an excellent education for all middle and high school students.* Washington, DC: Alliance for Excellent Education.

Jones, D. (2002, September 18). Businesses not feeling so charitable toward schools. *USA Today*, p. B1.

Kardos, S. M. (2003, April). *Integrated professional culture: Exploring new teachers' experiences in four states.* Paper presented at the annual meeting of the American Educational Research Association, Chicago.

Keller, B. (2000, February 2). Red ink in Newark mars state takeover. *Education Week, 19*(21), 1, 24.

Keller, B. (2003, April 30). Question of teacher turnover sparks research interest. *Education Week, XXII*(33), 8.

Kollars, D. (1998, September 6). When many kids drop out, state loses track [Electronic version]. *Sacramento Bee.* Retrieved June 4, 2003 from http://www.sacbee.com/news/projects/nobodys_kids/index.html.

Lemann, N. (1998, November). Ready, READ! *The Atlantic Monthly, 282*(5), 92–104.

LeTendre, G. K. (2000, August). *Downplaying choice: Institutionalized emotional norms in U.S. middle schools.* Paper presented at the annual meeting of the American Sociological Association, Washington, DC.

Lippman, L., Burns, S., McArthur, E., Burton, R., Smith, T., & Kaufman, P. (1996). *Urban schools: The challenge of location and poverty.* Washington, DC: National Center for Education Statistics (NCES No. 96-184).

Markley, M. (1996, December 1). Student self-discipline shifts burden for classroom order. *Houston Chronicle*, pp. 1A, 20A.

Martinez, M., & Klopott, S. (2002). *How is school reform tied to increasing college access and success for low-income and minority youth?* Washington, DC: Pathways to College Network Clearinghouse. Retrieved from http://www.pathwaystocollege.net/clearinghouse.

Mayer, D. P., Mullens, J. E., & Moore, M. T. (2000). *Monitoring school quality: An indicators report.* Washington, DC: U.S. Department of Education (NCES No. 2001030).

McDowell Group, Inc. (2001, November). *Report prepared for First Alaskans Foundation.* Anchorage, AK: Author.

McNeely, C. A., Nonnemaker, J., & Blum, R. (2002, April). Promoting school connectedness: Evidence from the National Longitudinal Study of Adolescent Health. *Journal of School Health, 72*(4), 138.

MDRC. (2001, December 10). *Memorandum to the Project GRAD Atlanta board of directors*, p. 5.

MetLife, Inc. (2001). *The MetLife survey of the American teacher: Key elements of quality schools.* New York: Author.

Modic, S. J. (Ed.). (1983, October 17). Excellence in management awards [Electronic version]. *Industry Week, 219*, 47–56. Retrieved Sept. 20, 2002 from http://garnet.acns.fsu.edu/~rlr0846/corp_legal_press/Tenneco/IndustryWk11-17-83.htm.

Mortenson, T. G. (2000, August). The human capital economy in Oregon, Washington, and California [Electronic version]. Retrieved July 6, 2004 from http://www.postsecondary.org. Paper presented to Ford Scholars, Bend, Oregon.

The National Center for Public Policy and Higher Education. (2000). *Losing ground: A national status report on the affordability of American higher education.* Washington, DC: Author.

Navarro, M. (2003, February 10). Education gap for Hispanics. *The New York Times*, p. A14.

New Jersey Department of Education. (2002). *2002 NCLB school report card.* Data retrieved Sept. 30, 2003 from http://education.state.nj.us/rc/nclb/13-3570-370.html.

Noeth, R. J., & Wimberly, G. L. (n.d.). *Creating seamless educational transitions for urban African American and Hispanic students.* Iowa City, IA: ACT Office of Policy Research.

O'Connell, D. (2002). Three that overcame the odds. *ENC Focus, 9*(4), 40.

Opuni, K. A. (1999). *Project GRAD 1998–99 Program Evaluation Report.* Houston: Project GRAD.

Opuni, K. A. (2001). *Project GRAD Evaluation Report: 1999–2000.* Houston: Project GRAD.

Opuni, K. A., & Ochoa, M. L. (2002a). *Project GRAD–Houston 2000–2001 program evaluation report: A chronicle of implementation benchmarks and achievements.* Houston, TX: University of St. Thomas Center for Research on School Reform.

Opuni, K. A., & Ochoa, M. L. (2002b). *Project GRAD–Houston 2001–2002 program evaluation report: An assessment of the Project GRAD model's effectiveness.* Houston, TX: University of St. Thomas Center for Research on School Reform.

Owings, J. (1995). *A profile of the American high school senior in 1992.* Washington, DC: U.S. Department of Education (NCES No. 95384).

Pathways to College Network. (2002). *How do educators' cultural belief systems affect underserved students' pursuit of postsecondary education?* Boston: Patricia George.

Peirce, N. (2002, January 2). *Challenges for big-city schools.* Washington, DC: Washington Post Writers Group.

Pitsch, M. (2003, October 27). Candidates are silent on college costs. *The Courier-Journal*, pp. A1, A4.

Pogrow, S. (2002, February). Success for All is a failure. *Phi Delta Kappan, 83*(6), 463–471.

Project GRAD–Atlanta. (2002). *Annual report.* Also, data retrieved from Atlanta Public Schools Web site, http://www.atlanta.k12.ga.us/parents_students/school_improvement/project_grad.html.

Reid, K. S. (2003, April 2). Achievement rising in urban districts, report finds. *Education Week, 22*(29), 3.

Romberg, T. A. (2002, Fall). 30 years of mathematics education research. *WCER Highlights, 14*(3), 2.

Sabulis, T. (2003, July 22). Passion for philanthropy drove others to give, serve. *The Atlanta Journal-Constitution.* Retrieved Sept. 30, 2003 from http://www.ajc.com/metro/content/0703/23brumley.html.

Selected AEIS Campus Data: A Multi-Year History for 1994–2002. (n.d.). [Marshall Middle School data file retrieved Oct. 12, 2003 from http://www.tea.state.tx.us.] Austin, TX: Texas Education Agency.

Shirley, D. (1997). *Community organizing for urban school reform.* Austin: University of Texas Press.

Slavin, R. E., & Madden, N. A. (1999). *Success for All/Roots & Wings: 1999 summary of research on achievement outcomes.* Baltimore: Johns Hopkins University, Center for Research on the Education of Students Placed At Risk.

Slavin, R. E., & Madden, N. A. (2001, April). *Reducing the gap: Success for All and the achievement of African-American and Hispanic students.* Paper presented at the annual meeting of the American Educational Research Association, Seattle.

Snipes, J., Doolittle, F., & Herlihy, C. (2002). *Foundations for success: Case studies of how urban school systems improve student achievement.* New York: MDRC.

Solmon, L. C., & Firetag, K. (2002, March 20). The road to teacher quality. *Education Week, 31*(27), 48.

Texas Education Agency. (2002). *2002 campus school report card.* [Data file retrieved Oct. 12, 2003 from http://www.tea.state.tx.us.] Austin, TX: Author.

Thomas B. Fordham Foundation. (2001, October). *The evolution of the New American Schools: From revolution to mainstream.* Washington, DC: Jeffrey Mirel.

Togneri, W., & Anderson, S. (2003). *Beyond islands of excellence: What districts can do to improve instruction and achievement in all schools.* Washington, DC: Learning First Alliance.

Ucelli, M. (2001, April 5). *From school improvement to systems reform.* Paper presented at the Rockefeller Foundation Symposium on Leveraging Change: An Emerging Framework for Educational Equity, Washington, DC.

U.S. Department of Education. (2000). *The condition of education 2000* (NCES No. 2000-062). Washington, DC: U.S. Government Printing Office.

U.S. Department of Education. (2003). *Overview and inventory of state education reforms: 1990 to 2000* (NCES No. 2003-020). Washington, DC: U.S. Government Printing Office.

Venezia, A., Kirst, M., & Antonio, A. (n.d.). *Betraying the college dream: How disconnected K–12 and postsecondary education systems undermine student aspirations.* Palo Alto, CA: Stanford University, the Stanford Institute for Higher Education Research.

Viadero, D. (2002, June 5). Study finds social barriers to advanced classes. *Education Week*, p. 5.

Wasley, P. A. (2003, Fall). In search of authentic reform. *Voices in Urban Education, 2*, 12–13.

Wilhelm, I. (2002, April 4). Foundation assets sag: Nation's largest grant makers see decline of 10 percent. [Electronic version]. *The Chronicle of Philanthropy.* Retrieved Oct. 23, 2002 from http://philanthropy.com/premium/articles/v14/i12/12000701.htm.

Winter, G. (2003, January 29). College loans rise, swamping graduates' dreams. *The New York Times*, p. A1.

INDEX

About the Author

Holly Holland, former editor of National Middle School Association's *Middle Ground* magazine, is the author or coauthor of four other books about education: *Making Change, The Heart of a High School, Champion for Student Success*, and *Making the Most of Middle School* (also by Teachers College Press). In addition to writing and editing articles, books, periodicals, and specialty publications for groups around the country, she has served on the board of the Kentucky Advisory Council for Gifted and Talented Education. She lives in Louisville with her husband, two sons, and a dog.